Thieves of Fire

Thieves of Fire

Denis Donoghue

New York
OXFORD UNIVERSITY PRESS
1974

'the liver gnawed by vultures,
though you brought fire to no one.'
KENNETH BURKE, *Towards a Better Life*

For Frances

Contents

Introduction: With Eliot in Mind   15

God with Thunder   33

The Peremptory Imagination   61

Thieves of Fire   87

Prometheus in Straits   111

Acknowledgements

I wish to thank the audience at the University of Kent for receiving, with patience and good-will, the T. S. Eliot Memorial Lectures delivered there in October and November 1972. I am especially grateful to friends and colleagues who subsequently carried the official theme into the Common Room of critical debate: R. A. Foakes, Ian Gregor, Mark Kinkead-Weekes. For many acts of kindness and most cordial hospitality I am deeply grateful to the Master of Eliot College, Professor F. S. L. Lyons, and to his gracious wife.

The first and the fourth of these lectures were printed, in slightly abbreviated form, in the Times Literary Supplement. *I am grateful to the Editor, Arthur Crook, for that amenity and for permission to reprint those lectures.*

D. D.

Introduction: With Eliot in Mind

THE T. S. Eliot Memorial Lectures for 1972 were delivered at the University of Kent in the week beginning October 30, the general title for the lectures being 'The Prome-theans'. My brief was to present in four lectures a theme answerable in some sense to Eliot's official interests; a theme, it might be, in poetry, drama, religion, criticism, philosophy, education, language, politics, or history. The lecturer was allowed so much freedom that he was hard put to know what to do with it. In the end, he consulted his own interests and hoped that his theme would be accepted as falling somewhere within the wide range of choices provided by the lectureship. The theme is the imagination in one of its aspects, and it appeared consistent, at least in principle, with Eliot's interest in describing the forms of imagination diversely embodied in Dante, in Shakespeare, and in the Metaphysical Poets. The lectures were prepared, then, as notes for a typology of the imagination; an attempt to describe certain types of imaginative action in literature and, among these, one in particular, which I call Promethean. The title, 'The Prometheans', did not prove entirely apt, mainly because it gave the impression that the writers I invoked to carry my theme were the only writers who exhibit this kind of imagination. The title seemed to say that the four writers, Milton, Blake, Melville, and Lawrence, exhausted a category by defining it. The new title, *Thieves of Fire*, gets over that difficulty, and it has the great merit of coming with Rimbaud's authority.

The lectures were not offered, indeed, as studies of four writers: those writers were presented as illustrations of an imaginative type or figure, and I stayed with each of them only for his acting in that character, and for as long as the going seemed good. My interest in the theme is consistent with my presenting it in four of its varia-tions; the theme is suggested by the variations, the only forms in which it is given. It is well to confess this sooner rather than later: for the time being, I am interested in these writers chiefly for the light they cast upon a certain kind of imagination. Sometimes I describe that imagination by contrasting it with another kind which acts upon a different faith; the same procedure holds on those occasions, too, my aim is not to do full justice to the several writers or to register the diversity of their works but to call them as witnesses to a particular character of the imagination. In practice, this makes for a duality of imaginative types, and there are strong precedents for such a thing. Wörringer would not have gone far with 'abstraction' without recourse to 'empathy'; Nietzsche has Dionysiac clamour answered, successfully or not, by Apollonian order; Jung's *Psychological Types* is largely a description of two, introspective and extrovert. If you emphasize one aspect, you are bound to look at its opposite.

As for the method of proceeding: the lecture, as a form, is not the most suitable occasion for engaging with the detail of a poem or a novel, it goes better with a general view and a tangible argument. The relation between detail and argument is always difficult for the lecturer, and he is likely to settle upon one or the other as a desperate preference. It seemed to me on this occasion that the theme required me to proceed on a certain level of abstraction some distance above that of explication or 'practical criticism' and yet to assume that a good deal of fairly close reading had already been undertaken, as if by way of homework before the lectures. While the theme called for a certain altitude, it also supposed as a shared possession between lecturer and audience a fairly lively sense of the detail of certain works. The lecturer consulted his own temper, then, in indulging himself in a somewhat expansive mood, turning at times toward reverie and meditation. The risk in such indulgence was a possible breach of decorum: even a listener of generous disposition might think the lecturer's tone too rhapsodic to be decent. At the same time I was bound to think the theme an exalted matter and to believe that it could only be fulfilled in a style, as Shelley said, 'in itself music and persuasion': gross failure to achieve such a style, in the event, would not refute the belief, it would merely leave it famished.

I was also mindful of the fact that the audience assembled for the 1972 series of Eliot Lectures would reasonably expect the lectures to take the form of literary criticism. It is difficult to define this activity or to fix a limit to its direction. Even if we agree that 'practical criticism' is its centre, we still dispute the location of its circumference. When we speak of 'literary criticism as we know it', we usually mean 'as I like it'. So I had to ask the audience at

Canterbury, by implication, to let me run on a loose rein, and to give me perhaps inordinate latitude. I did not want to be held too strictly to account for my movements or to show that they were at every point compatible with the common understanding of literary criticism. I felt justified in this errancy, at least in principle, by considering that many of the critics I most admire have taken all the latitude in the world, and have earned the right to such freedom by the extraordinary power of their perceptions, many of them being achieved by critical reverie. I mean the sublimists, from Longinus to Bachelard, Blackmur, and Benjamin. It will be understood that I risk naming such critics only to say that literary criticism is more fluid in its procedures and determinations than the phrase 'as we know it' implies. I do not think we lose anything by saying that criticism is as various as critics, or that it is a country noted for liberality and tolerance.

In its simplest version, the myth of Prometheus tells a story to account for the origin of human consciousness. Prometheus stole it from Zeus and gave it as a gift to men, ostensibly in the form of fire. I want to say a word or two about its nature as a gift. Emerson has an essay on gifts, and the anthropologist Marcel Mauss has a famous book on the subject, but I do not find in either of those places an account of the special category of gifts in which the given object has been stolen. This is surprising, because a stolen gift is surrounded by an entirely different set of connotations from those which surround the innocent gift. A gift of any kind starts a cycle of obligation: this is Marcel Mauss's theme. Emerson says that flowers are always appropriate gifts 'because they are a proud assertion that a ray of beauty outvalues all the utilities of the world',[1] and I assume that the donor wants to share something of that sentiment with his friend. Obligations are incurred and returned. But a gift which has been stolen is a much more complex matter because it cannot release itself from its origin in violence, risk, and guilt; the receiver is incriminated in the donor's crime. What kind of obligation is incurred by a man who accepts a stolen

---

[1] Emerson, *Works*, edited by A. C. Hearn. Edinburgh. Nimmo, Hay, and Mitchell, 1907, p. 188.

gift? In an innocent gift, two people are joined in a relation, but in a stolen gift there are three, the third being the original owner, who is related to the receiver through the thief. Emerson says that in the ideal gift you give your friend something that properly belongs to his character, and what you choose to give should also belong to your own. That is why a gift is imperfect if we merely buy it. 'The only gift is a portion of thyself,' Emerson says; 'Thou must bleed for me'. Prometheus's gift, although outrageous in its theft, is proper on other counts: proper to the receiver, because it testifies to his character in its potentiality if not in its present nature: and proper to the donor because it is a part of him, his divine superiority in knowledge. The interest of the myth consists in the ambiguity with which it surrounds the lucidity of knowledge, the moral darkness from which its brightness came. When we call it a myth, we mean that it is a genre of feeling; not feeling in itself, but one of its categories. The myth of Prometheus begins as a story, an anecdote of transgression, but because many generations have found it significant it has become a category, one of the available forms of feeling. Of course it rarely works by itself, normally it is employed along with other genres of feeling, some of which are sufficiently well known to have names, but others not. One of the problems of discussing the Promethean way of feeling is that we have to isolate it from other ways, for convenience and lucidity, and by doing so we distort it, as if we were to print some chapters of a book in italics. There is no help for this situation, and we cannot even promise to bear it constantly in mind. 'There is no thought which embraces all our thought.'[1] One of the deficiencies of anything is that it is not also something else. However, with that disclaimer, my theme is the Promethean mode in literature, the sense of literature as propelled by motives for which Prometheus is a reasonably accurate name. The writers with whom I am chiefly concerned are chosen mainly to illustrate the Promethean mode and sometimes to qualify it. I have recourse to other writers for contrast and comparison.

---

[1] M. Merleau-Ponty, *Phenomenology of Perception*, translated by Colin Smith. London. Routledge and Kegan Paul, 1962, p. xiv.

Introduction: With Eliot in Mind

I should mention, incidentally, and sooner rather than later, that the writers I have chosen to discuss were all, in one degree or another, alien to T. S. Eliot: he was either indifferent or hostile to them. I cannot recall that he ever said anything about Melville, though he was concerned with American literature, being an American poet, and he had a good deal to say about Poe, Whitman, Hawthorne, Henry James, Mark Twain, Emerson and other compatriots. His relation to Milton is still a matter of critical dispute, but no one denies that the relation was difficult and somewhat abrasive. Eliot found Milton's works standing in his way, he could not circumvent them, and chose instead to strike his talent against them. Later, with his own work more or less completely achieved, he confronted Milton again in a more patient spirit. But it was never a genial relation. Milton was always, to Eliot, what Eliot is to contemporary poets, a formidable presence, a Master. Again, Eliot's relation to Blake was harsh; he agreed with the common opinion that Blake was a genius, but he did not consider that a genius was the greatest or best thing a man could be, and there are moments in Eliot's meditations upon this question when he appears to say that genius is no excuse for failing to be a classic poet or, better still, a saint. There is something disreputable in being merely a genius, according to Eliot, if it is a matter of choice. So Eliot wrote of D. H. Lawrence with distaste, on the whole: in every paragraph there are sentences of appreciation, he spoke of Lawrence as 'a profound explorer of human nature', there are many comments of this kind, but there is always an implication of pride and perversity in Lawrence's work which Eliot found hard to forgive. In the end, on the occasion of the trial of *Lady Chatterley's Lover*, Eliot moved to defend the book and to speak more appreciatively of Lawrence than he had ever spoken before, but his sense of Lawrence's art as alien, on the whole, persisted. I shall comment later upon these relations, but in the meantime it is enough that Eliot is a critical presence when we discuss Promethean writers, we cannot avoid being aware of his severity. This is bound to be a help, because otherwise there is a risk that we may let these powerful writers run away with the show: they are all major rhetoricians, and they demand from the reader a much more extreme response than he is accustomed to give.

If we ask why these writers are alien to Eliot, it is also a way of asking why they are alien to many other readers whose sense of literature Eliot expressed. We cannot say that Eliot's response was eccentric. He sensed in such writers, I suggest, a quality of wilfulness, intractability, amounting in particular cases to heresy. When he was engaged with the question of orthodoxy, which is the question of tradition in another idiom, he found these writers heretical, victims of the heresy of private judgment. Whatever official beliefs they held, they believed in themselves to the degree that no other belief could be compared with that, for intensity and vehemence. Eliot detected this element, and found it overbearing. With Dante and Shakespeare as exemplars, he found the Promethean writers somewhat provincial; even Milton, though Eliot does not use the word in writing of that poet.

But it is invidious to use the criterion of orthodoxy, as Eliot used it, when the occasion is literary. It has not worn well as a term in literary criticism; most readers probably think it an improper criterion, if 'tradition' or 'classicism' answer just as well. Without using any of these terms, it is possible to point to a certain truculence in Promethean writers in the relation they declare between mind and experience. It is not characteristic of them to place their minds at the service of experience, even with a view to understanding it. Such writers demand a relation to experience which we call dynamic if we want to praise it, and insistent if we distrust it. We feel this demand as an essential element in these writers, especially when we think of other writers who do not make anything of the kind; when we contrast Milton with George Herbert, or Blake with Wordsworth, or even Lawrence with Joyce. Let me give as examples two poems in which the speakers are calling upon God for justice in the form of vengeance. The first is Milton's sonnet 'On the Late Massacre in Piemont', the occasion being the 'Piemontese Easter' massacre of the Waldensians, a heretical sect, on April 24, 1655:

> Avenge O Lord thy slaughter'd Saints, whose bones
> Lie scatter'd on the Alpine mountains cold,
> Ev'n them who kept thy truth so pure of old

When all our Fathers worship't Stocks and Stones,
Forget not: in thy book record their groanes
   Who were thy Sheep and in their antient Fold
   Slayn by the bloody Piemontese that roll'd
   Mother with Infant down the Rocks. Their moans
The Vales redoubl'd to the Hills, and they
   To Heav'n. Their martyr'd blood and ashes sow
   O're all th'Italian fields where still doth sway
The triple Tyrant: that from these may grow
   A hunder'd-fold, who having learnt thy way
   Early may fly the Babylonian wo.[1]

Clearly, Milton is not merely saying, with whatever degree of rhetorical force, 'God, help the Italian Protestants to beat the Pope'. Nor is he content to protect the memory of the slaughtered saints, though the first quatrain has the effect of enclosing them and their ancestors within the power of the imperative verbs, 'Avenge' and 'Forget not'. His feeling includes the assertion that God as the Good Shepherd should have looked after His flock, and should not have allowed His enemies to slaughter them. 'In thy book record their groanes / Who were thy Sheep'; the record is pathetic, and its absurdity is meant to reflect back upon the defaulting shepherd who let the slaughter happen. Recording the groans in a divine book comes a poor second to Nature's response, which was at least quick enough to send the noises of death to heaven. So Milton feels himself justified in demanding a special effort from God now, to make up for such a feeble performance. He must do at least as well as Cadmus, multiplying by 100 the Protestants drawn against 'the triple Tyrant'. Some of this feeling comes again in the 'two-handed engine' passage in *Lycidas*, and in both cases what we respond to is Milton's truculence, his setting aside one kind of propriety in favour of a more daring kind, more Asiatic than Attic; and in any event he stakes everything upon his own sensibility.

Herbert's poem is 'Decay':

---

[1] *Poems of Mr. John Milton*, edited by Cleanth Brooks and John Edward Hardy. London. Dennis Dobson, 1957, p. 291.

Sweet were the days when thou didst lodge with Lot,
  Struggle with Jacob, sit with Gideon,
Advise with Abraham; when thy power could not
  Encounter Moses' strong complaints and mone.
    Thy words were then, *Let me alone.*

One might have sought and found thee presently
  At some fair oak, or bush, or cave, or well.
Is my God this way? No, they would reply,
  He is to Sinai gone as we heard tell
    List, ye may heare great Aaron's bell.

But now thou dost thyself immure and close
  In some one corner of a feeble heart,
Where yet both Sinne and Satan, thy old foes,
  Do pinch and straiten thee and use much art
    To gain thy thirds and little part.

I see the world grows old, whenas the heat
  Of thy great love once spread, as in an urn
Doth closet up itself and still retreat,
  Cold sinne still forcing it, till it return
    And calling Justice, all things burn.[1]

What is remarkable in this poem is not Herbert's use of domestic figures to express metaphysical relations, but the confidence with which he uses them; his assumption that whatever he wants to say can be entrusted to these homely terms. There may be feelings which require a more theatrical form of expression, but Herbert eschews them, not because he cannot imagine them but because he chooses to leave them alone. He is content with ready procedures and with the range of feeling which they allow. So he hands his feeling over to the language, and is happy to abide by its determination. Eliot has pointed out that Herbert appears to have been a man of haughty disposition, not at all placid or comfortable. This is true. But he was nevertheless willing to confine himself, as a poet, to whatever feeling could be conveyed by an equable language, a domestic music. The present poem moves by a tech-

---

[1] Herbert, *Works*, edited by F. E. Hutchinson, second edition, Oxford. Clarendon Press, 1945, p. 512.

nique of willing postponement, so that the extraordinary last line, the burning of all things, comes as if it were in the nature of the case. It is extraordinary as an extension of the ordinary, not as an affront to it. Its most powerful quality is the impression it gives of being merely the logical conclusion of premises quietly laid down, step by step. Herbert speaks as if he were a mere logician, charting the progress of a logic which he is content to recite. His indicative moods have the force of imperatives, but not their characteristic clamour: the last imperative comes as if released from a situation that compelled it, it does not come as an explosion of personal feeling, but as the last touch of the logic. The poem is personal, almost colloquial, but the speaker makes no claim on his own behalf, he is merely the servant of its reason. He is content to let the fortunes of his feeling coincide with the fortunes of his language: the magnificence of the last sentence, coinciding with the contours of the stanza from beginning to end, arises from the confidence which the speaker reposes in the language in which he participates. He does not claim anything more for himself than participation in a common language: what he means is what the language allows him to mean, he does not register any higher claim.

The juxtaposition of these poems involves the juxtaposition of two different attitudes to experience; two different notions of the relation between mind and experience. Generalizing somewhat, we can say that in Promethean writers there is always a certain tension between feeling and form, or between story and style. The writer always wants either a special language, devoted to his sole purpose, or a common language willing to be driven hard. If he is a novelist, very little of his feeling is given in the mere story, most of it depends upon amplifications or qualifications imposed upon the story. If he is a poet, he is likely to demand that the language give up some of its common qualities in favour of his; or emphasize affiliations somewhat foreign to its nature. Above all, such writers refuse to accept that in practice the limits of the language determine the possibilities of their feeling. Some writers, like Herbert, are ready to accept the verdict of the language, that not everything is reasonable and natural. The Promethean writers resent such interference. If their feeling is in excess of the available language, they drive the language to make up for the difference.

This complicates the matter because it recognizes the declared presence of 'personality' even in the formal nature of the work of art. In Promethean writers, it is hard to separate the formal nature of the work from the personality of the poet, his charisma. Max Weber used this term to register the presence of exceptional forces in society, especially in certain people whose lives are surrounded by a halo or aura of presence. We speak of the radiance or the reverberation of such people. In reading Promethean writers we have the impression that they feel themselves participating in an ancestral drama not limited to their own: their works are at once immediate and distant, these battles are taking place now and always. We feel that these writers have absorbed of the past mainly its trouble, and that in the present version of the quarrel their private feeling spills over the available forms. So it is common to say of each that his most achieved work is himself, his identity as victim-hero of the ancestral drama: the self in question determines whatever is visible and actual in the work, but it is not fulfilled by the work, there is a remainder, an incorrigible excess which is visible only in the name. There is a sense in which the name 'D. H. Lawrence' means more, has more charismatic aura, than anything in the fiction he wrote; a sense in which the fiction, however we respond to it, is merely one of the more or less exhaustive forms of his life. Literary criticism has nothing to say of charisma, except to feel embarrassed in its presence: this is a good reason for keeping the boundaries of criticism without exact definition, we never know when we will want to run wild, trying to catch effects not directly visible in the works. I think Eliot felt this difficulty in thinking of Lawrence, and that it forced him into the excess of denying, on one occasion, that Lawrence was an artist at all. Eliot knew that Lawrence was a charismatic personality, he said he was a medicine man rather than an artist; not an artist 'but a man with a sketch-book'.[1] He thought *Sons and Lovers* a 'rather sickly and

[1] John Baillie and Hugh Martin (editors), *Revelation,* by Gustaf Aulen, Karl Barth, Sergius Bulgakoff, M. C. D'Arcy, T. S. Eliot, Walter M. Horton, and William Temple. London. Faber and Faber, 1937, p. 30.

morally unintelligible book',[1] and he agreed with Wyndham Lewis's attack on Lawrence, in *Paleface*, as a victim of sentimentality and primitivism, a worshipper of stocks and stones. But he could not refute the personality, of which the works were a declared part. This may account for the frequency with which he recurred to a writer he found distasteful. It may also account for our impression that the faults of Promethean writers do not much matter. It may be a cause of scandal to I. A. Richards that Lawrence did not take solar physics seriously and wrote of the sun as if physics did not exist; but very few other readers are scandalized, they take Lawrence's neo-physics in their stride, as they take Milton's cosmology, or Blake's prophetic paradigms. I am not equating these objects of attention or blurring the distinctions which should be made between them; I am merely suggesting that readers are not troubled by them. What Lawrence writes of the sun is bad physics, but as the vehicle of his feeling, it is irrefutable: its truth is the personal rhythm of the sentences.

This is what we keep coming back to, a personal rhythm which establishes certain writers as cousins in spirit, despite a multitude of overt differences. The Promethean feeling is a sense of the risk of experience, and a determination to maintain such a life by force of will. It is proper to say of the Promethean intervention in human history that it was a once-for-all affair, as a result of which we know we can't go home again: the intervention is historical and irrevocable, its chief characteristic is that it cannot be deleted. Theft of the divine fire of knowledge made reflection possible and therefore necessary; it made men self-aware, self-conscious, it made the human race a multitude of reflexive animals. But because the gift of consciousness is stolen, it introduces division into consciousness itself, as a mark of guilt, the 'unhappy consciousness' which Hegel describes in the *Phenomenology of the Spirit*. Consciousness is stolen fruit or stolen fire, in either form the original sin, source of a correspondingly original guilt. Men take the harm out of it by converting some of its energy to a pious end, the knowledge of God, or its secular form, the knowledge of Nature. But forgiveness

---

[1] *Ibid.*, p. 30.

is never complete. One of the consequences of the theft is that man knows his attributes and is guilty in possessing them. The reflexiveness of mind, which is in one sense its glory, is in another a token of its criminality, its transgression at the source. This is why many modern poets have longed for an ignorant audience, as if to redeem their own self-consciousness, making mind innocent again. But the theft also gave men the power and the habit of self-expression by recourse to symbols; it allowed them to use symbols to mediate between two kinds of experience lately sundered – nature and man, or as we would now say, nature and culture. Symbols are at once natural and human, natural in their origin, human in their use and meaning. Above all, Prometheus made possible the imaginative enhancement of experience, the metaphorical distinction between what happens to us and what we make of the happening. That is to say, Prometheus provided men with consciousness as the transformational grammar of experience. No wonder the gift also gave men a sense of the endlessness of possibility arising from the endlessness of knowledge and desire. The power of symbolism helped men to maintain a relation between themselves and nature, or at least to devise new rituals of relation to replace the old intimacy, but it did not bring peace between men and gods. The sources do not tell us much of the relation between the human race and the god Zeus after the theft of fire; they are preoccupied with the punishment imposed on the thief, and the eventual reconciliation between Zeus and Prometheus. There is no evidence that Zeus thought any the better of men for their new skills. The imagination has always been a contentious power, as a result, so far as men are concerned in their relations with the gods. A typology of the imagination would be an explication of the several ways in which men have risen above themselves by the possession of consciousness. The Promethean imagination is only the most extreme gesture in that account, and it is not alone in featuring arbitrary defiance in men, a show of force in the gods answered by a show of blasphemy in men. The predicament remains: imagination, the divine power in men, falsely acquired, stolen from the gods in the first of many similar outrages. Since then, the Promethean imagination has always been defiant: it starts with an incorrigible sense of its own power, and seeks in nature only the means of its fulfilment. Whatever it fastens upon must relinquish itself, capitulate if necessary to the imagination; it is merely a means to an end. The end is the imagination's disclosure of its own power; the mind certifies itself. The Promethean imagination does not begin with any respect for 'the Other': specific objects of attention are valued only in default of other objects, and there is a sense in which all objects are interchangeable. Or, to put it more precisely, the imagination does not allow objects to assert themselves or to hold out for their right. They have no right, except to be useful. No object is ever allowed to mark an outer limit of the Promethean imagination: on the contrary, limits are observed only to be transcended.

I am describing two types of imagination, featuring two different attitudes to experience. Both ways have implications for the relation between the mind and experience, or between the mind and the materials with which it engages. The easiest paradigm comes from sculpture, where the artist working directly upon his materials is a concentrated image of man dealing with his experience. Adrian Stokes has provided the terms for two different artistic procedures, and they chime exactly with the two attitudes I am describing. He distinguishes between the motives involved in carving and in modelling, where carving is concerned with the release of significance deemed already to exist, imprisoned in the stone, and modelling is a more plastic process by which the sculptor imposes his meaning upon the stone. In carving, the artist assumes that the block of stone contains within itself the form invented for it by nature; the artist's desire is merely to liberate that form, to disclose its hidden face, to reveal the truth on the stone by a light 'as if from inside it'. In modelling, on the other hand, the artist gives the stone his own truth, or what he insists is his own truth; the truth of the stone as a different truth is not acknowledged. The modeller 'imbues spatial objects with the animus and calculation of inner life', meaning his own inner life. He projects his feeling into the stone which he understands as dead until that moment: it comes to life as a manifestation of his life. He works the miracle of bringing a dead thing to life by giving it his own life: he can do it because his life of feeling is endless, sustained by desire. I should report that Adrian Stokes has committed himself to a preference, as between these two imaginative attitudes to the natural object. He prefers, he says, works of art 'conceived primarily from the carving side', because he values especially 'the meaning conveyed by the accentuated otherness, by the self-subsistence, as it were, of forms, rather than by those juxtapositions through which we are made vividly conscious of tensions of the mind'. 'I have more concern,' he says, 'with restoration, reparation, than with the versatile interior giants that seem to infect the artist's material with shadowy or stark power.'[1] The writers whom I think of as Prometheans are versatile giants in that sense, and I hope to say something about the tensions of the mind which their writings exhibit. I should also mention that a few years ago in a book called *The Ordinary Universe* I tried to set out a preference for certain writers whose works are conceived primarily from the carving side. But I found myself fending off the versatile giants, trying not to notice their presence, so that my carving writers would have all the show to themselves. It was as if, offering to say something about Christianity, I identified that faith with the temper of St. Francis of Assisi, and tried for the moment not to recognize the presence of St. Augustine. On the present occasion, I mean to bring the different traditions more closely together, and to attend to one without banishing the other. In literature, to speak of carvers and modellers is justifiable if we recognize that we are pointing to extreme definitions, and that in practice the motives at work are likely to be mixed. It may be true as a working generalization that modern literature exhibits for the most part a belief in the peremptory imagination, and that modern readers are persuaded to value most highly those writers whose fictions would be most insufferable if they were to be transformed into practice and fact. But there are carvers at work, too, and the motives of the carver often assert themselves in a writer whose primary allegiance is to the modelling side.

---

[1] Richard Wollheim (editor), *The Image in Form: Selected Writings of Adrian Stokes*. Harmondsworth. Penguin Books, 1972, pp. 48, 59, 69.

Perhaps the most extreme heresy among Promethean writers is their assumption that the Promethean intervention is the whole story of human life, that nothing else matters. The story is extraordinarily compelling, and it is possible to insist upon its significance to the point of excluding virtually every other factor. I am pleased to find this exorbitance rebuked in at least one of the early accounts, the *Protagoras* of Plato. According to this version, the gods, having created men and animals compounded of earth and fire, instructed Epimetheus and Prometheus to provide these new creatures with appropriate faculties. Epimetheus started first by giving the animals the diverse means of protecting themselves, but he left himself short of faculties necessary to men. Then Prometheus, seeing that the first men were naked and defenceless, stole fire and its wisdom and gave the gift to men. I interpret the gift as including language. The new race was now in a position to maintain itself from day to day. But each man lived apart from the others and, a Hobbesian before Hobbes, looked upon his kind as enemies; he had to defend himself not only against the wilder animals but against his neighbours. Men did not live together in communities, did not make cities, did not understand that a society might be made. Protagoras reports this by saying that although men acquired from Prometheus the skills of daily life they still lacked 'civic wisdom', which remained in Zeus's possession. When they tried to form themselves into communities, they failed, and quarrelled to death among themselves. According to this version, Zeus was touched with pity for men, despite his sense of outrage, and Protagoras reports that Zeus sent Hermes to make up for Prometheus's deficiency, or rather to complete the work which he had impiously begun. Hermes brought to men, therefore, the civic art of justice and order, that they might live peacefully together on earth.

I take this version as a salutary rebuke to the Prometheans, and I think it will permit some reasonable application to the writers in question, and especially to Lawrence. It may be said of Lawrence that he wanted not the world but its beginning: he was enraged because he was not present at the start of human experience. In his later fiction he wrote as if he hoped to destroy most of what he saw in human life, and nearly everything he saw in human society, in favour of what he sensed beneath the corrupt appearances. He was content with the animal and botanical worlds: no flower had ever insulted him, or stood in the way of his freedom. These are the worlds of his poetry. But he was angry with the human world because it would not let him begin again, or start a new life under the auspices of Father, Son, and Holy Ghost. His predicament is shadowed in the breakdown of the relation between Prometheus, Hermes, and Zeus. Hermes testifies to the deficiency of Prometheus, he brings to men those arts which depend not upon the thinker in his lonely tower but upon the same thinker in community, debate, politics, trade, and travel. Hermes is Zeus's messenger, and what he brings is a gift from Zeus, but in his own character he testifies to the social impulse. It is well known that Lawrence, partly under the stimulation of the social psychologist Trigant Burrow, came to value this impulse and to think it fundamental, but he always believed that the crowd is even more neurotic than the individual, and that in any event one must start with the individual. The good society is a possibility, an ideal image. If Prometheus stands for the pleasures and pains of individual consciousness, Hermes accounts for the possibility of values in common, the sharing of knowledge, the idea of a society. What Zeus stands for is divine power as the source of everything, the ground of all beseechings.

God with Thunder

THE *Prometheus Bound* of Aeschylus ends with the hero vanishing from sight amid thunder and lightning. It is assumed that the play was one of three, but its companions are lost. That the extant play was the first part of the trilogy is now widely agreed: the second was probably a *Prometheus Unbound*, and the third a *Prometheus Firekindler*, though Professor Lloyd-Jones has recently suggested that the third may have been the *Women of Etna*.[1] The gist of the drama is that Prometheus stole fire from Zeus and brought it as a dangerous gift to mankind. In the end, he is somewhat mysteriously reconciled to his master. We do not see these offences or reconciliations enacted, we see Prometheus bound upon a rock, we hear claims and recriminations, until Zeus sends his thunderbolt. The story is not complete, but we allow what we have of it to seize our imaginations: so far as we are concerned, we have seen Prometheus dauntless, and we have seen him overwhelmed. He remains in our minds as a notable gesture, a style of defiance, resistance brought to the end of the line; and since he has been a friend to man, we think him justified in everything, not least in the quality of his defeat. It is difficult to take Zeus's part in such a conflict. The mythologists tell us that Prometheus and Zeus are eventually reconciled; this is natural, since neither of them can be finally defeated, and reconciliation is implicit in the form of a trilogy. We are free to suppose a reconciliation, and only a little less free to suppose an alternative ending. The poet A. D. Hope has a poem in which he imagines Prometheus released, but released to the torment of contemplating what men have done with the fire he stole on their behalf. Zeus's words are:

> Go, set the Titan free;
> And let his torment be to wander wide
> The ashes of mankind from sea to sea,
> Judging that theft of fire from which they died.[2]

---

[1] Hugh Lloyd-Jones, *The Justice of Zeus*. Berkeley and Los Angeles. University of California Press, 1971, p. 102.
[2] A. D. Hope, 'Prometheus Unbound'. *Collected Poems 1930-1965*. London. Hamish Hamilton, 1966, p. 89.

Wallace Stevens said that 'to see the gods dispelled in mid-air and dissolve like clouds is one of the great human experiences', but he also said of the gods that they were 'a part of the glory of the earth'. 'In the presence of the gods, or of their images, we are in the presence of perfection in created beings.'[1] That is one reason why 'the death of Satan was a tragedy / For the imagination',[2] because men withdrew belief and thereby dispersed one of their own grand creations. Prometheus is to us a name, what he names is an attitude, a way of life, embodied to the degree of perfection. He was probably a minor god among Greek divinities, and certainly minor in comparison with Zeus, but we do not allow this consideration to reduce him in our eyes: he is not a minor figure to us. If we look for him apart from Aeschylus's play and a few other places, we find him in a certain quality of imagination. My interest in the transmission of the Promethean myth is incidental to another interest, that of recognizing the hero in the imagination of certain writers who may or may not proclaim him directly. I am interested in describing a certain kind of imagination as Promethean. Let us assume that we are in a world dear to Stevens, where men having taken the place of gods and demigods think their own imaginations divine, with consequences not yet exhausted. We are concerned with the consequences when we speak of individualism, freedom, pride, the figure of the modern hero, and reality as a mere function of the imagination. We are concerned with imaginations which, in one degree or another, have taken the place of Prometheus. If we have seen Prometheus dispelled in mid-air, we have also seen his spirit animating the imagination of certain writers, and the proof is their style, their way of addressing themselves to reality. I begin with Milton, a poet in whom the question of divinity is also the question of mankind, and both are questions of imagination.

About halfway through the fourth Book of *Paradise Lost* we come to the Garden, and an elaborate description follows of the 'blissful bower' of Adam and Eve, a mosaic of flowers. Milton's

[1] Wallace Stevens, *Opus Posthumous*. New York. Knopf, 1957, pp. 206, 207, 212.
[2] Stevens, *Collected Poems*. London. Faber and Faber, 1955, p. 319.

way of registering the plenitude of the nuptial setting is to invoke certain mythological comparisons, including 'universal Pan', and to say that Eve's bower beggared such images, fact exceeding fiction:

> Here in close recess
> With flowers, garlands, and sweet-smelling herbs
> Espoused Eve decked first her nuptial bed,
> And heavenly choirs the hymenean sung,
> What day the genial angel to our sire
> Brought her in naked beauty more adorned,
> More lovely than Pandora, whom the gods
> Endowed with all their gifts, and O too like
> In sad event, when to the unwiser son
> Of Japhet brought by Hermes, she ensnared
> Mankind with her fair looks, to be avenged
> On him who had stole Jove's authentic fire.[1]

The sentence would have been long enough for most poets if it had ended with the comparison of Eve and Pandora in point of beauty. Milton puts at risk the intimations of beauty and opulence by following up the comparison to its 'sad event' in both cases. Eve is compared to Pandora, and therefore Adam to 'the unwiser son of Japhet', Epimetheus, Prometheus's brother, a comparison enforced by calling Epimetheus 'mankind'. Milton lets the comparison run to Prometheus and 'Jove's authentic fire', looking forward to an equally sad event and vengeance no less severe. He is a poet of risk, he allows his sentence to take every risk of incrimination. He is not protective toward his verses. There is nothing to prevent the reader from thinking of Eve as brought to Adam in punishment for some aboriginal offence, symbolically re-enacted by Adam, as though Eve were the embodiment of one disaster and the cause of another. T. S. Eliot said that he always felt embarrassed when he tried to visualize the scene in the Garden, and he advised readers not to try too hard. But the imagination at work in Milton's sentence is dramatic rather than visual or aural, because of

---

[1] Milton, *Paradise Lost*, IV.708–19: *The Poems of John Milton*, eds. John Carey and Alastair Fowler. London. Longmans, 1968, pp. 654–6.

the latitude of risk which it incurs, starting with flowers and ending with fire. Milton is afraid of nothing that the recital may bring, even if a shadow of the sad event falls back upon the ostensibly happy Garden. He allows the sentence to do its worst, like the comparison itself, ending in fire and vengeance. We begin to recognize a particular form of imagination at work, an imagination ready to give offence.

Nearly everything we feel about Prometheus comes from Aeschylus and Shelley; nearly everything we know of him comes from Hesiod and Apollodorus. The story, so far as it is told in Hesiod's *Theogony* and *Works and Days*, amplified by Apollodorus's *Library*, is soon told; it is suggestive rather than complex. Ignoring minor discrepancies, we can say that Prometheus, a demigod, sometimes appears as the creator of mankind, but sometimes only as mankind's benefactor: if creator, he moulded men out of water and earth; if benefactor, he thwarted Zeus's design of bringing the human race to an end and starting all over again in some other form. At the foundation feast Prometheus deceived Zeus by giving him the mere bones of an ox to eat, tricked out with shining fat, while to men he gave the genuine meat. In anger, Zeus refused to give men the fire they needed for their development. But Prometheus stole it, concealed it in a stalk of fennel, and gave it to men. In return, Zeus gave men, as Hesiod says, 'an evil thing in which they may all be glad of heart while they embrace their own destruction':[1] obviously a woman, accepted by the foolish brother Epimetheus in the form of Pandora. Prometheus is chained to a rock while Hephaestus drives a wedge through his chest. Every day an eagle swoops upon him and devours the lobes of his liver, which grow again by night. At last, Prometheus is reconciled to Zeus, having matched himself in wit with the son of Cronos, Chiron; whereupon Heracles kills the eagle.

Prometheus is one who knows in advance, Epimetheus one who learns afterwards, when it is too late. The comparison of Epimetheus with Adam is therefore easy and natural, but comparisons

---

[1] Hesiod, *Works and Days: Hesiod, The Homeric Hymns, and Homerica*, tr. Hugh G. Evelyn-White. Loeb edition, 1920, p. 7.

with Prometheus are more complex. He is like Satan in one respect, like Christ in another; a rebel against the great god, and a friend to man, a scapegoat for man's sake. Unlike Christ, Prometheus never appears as a man, but he makes common cause with humanity without sharing human nature. Goethe saw him as Lord of the Earth. He is intimate with the elements, and this is perhaps the source of his secret knowledge. He knew from the start what his role would be, and the suffering he would undergo, so it is easy to translate him into Christian terms, a translation effected with little strain by Tertullian. But Prometheus's double nature is always acknowledged; as by Coleridge who said that he was the Redeemer and the Devil jumbled together.

As for Zeus's authentic fire, presumably Milton called it authentic in the sense of 'original', meaning that when it was stolen it was desecrated, torn from its first source. In Aeschylus's play Prometheus claims to have given mankind not only fire but nearly everything else as well, identifying fire with nearly every value. He claims to have given man the power of reason, the several arts of number, writing, carpentry, boat-building, astronomy, divination, astrology, medicine, metallurgy, indeed 'every art possessed by man'.[1] Milton would not have given Prometheus full marks for this, because he regarded most of the arts invented since the Fall as necessary evils, and he made Raphael take a superior line when Adam enquired about such matters. Prometheus also claims to have given men hope, so that, unlike himself, they would not foresee their fate. But fire is ambiguous and diverse, as Bachelard shows in *La Psychanalyse de feu* and *La Flamme d'une chandelle*. There was no such thing in the Garden of Eden, the discovery of fire was one of the consequences of the Fall, as Milton makes clear in Books IX and X of *Paradise Lost*. In Book VI Satan, his army temporarily subdued, invents gunpowder and firearms in answer to God's thunder. If all the arts are necessary, as Milton implies, to repair some of the damage caused by the Fall, the arts sponsored by fire are at once dangerous and thrilling. Kerenyi, speaking of the dark-

---

[1] Aeschylus, *Prometheus Bound*, tr. H. Weir Smyth. Loeb edition, I, pp. 214–314 (line 506).

ness associated with Prometheus, says that it signifies 'the deficiency of one who needs fire in order to achieve a more perfect form of being. In obtaining this higher form of being for man, Prometheus shows himself to be man's double, an eternal image of man's basically imperfect form of being'.[1] The association of fire with deficiency, challenge, and risk is clear. Even when it is interpreted in benign terms, on the whole, there is always a sense of its danger, and the price to be paid for its theft. Coleridge identifies the Promethean fire with intelligence, which Milton in *Paradise Lost* calls 'sanctity of reason' (VII. 508). Prometheus stole on man's behalf the divine spark, meaning in Coleridge's language 'reason theoretical and practical'. 'By a transition ordinary even in allegory, and appropriate to mythic symbol, but especially significant in the present case – the transition, I mean, from the giver to the gift – the giver, in very truth, being the gift, "whence the soul receives reason; and reason is her being", says our Milton. Reason is from God, and God is reason, *mens ipsissima.*'[2] Coleridge cannot be expected to think the cost of such a gift exorbitant, but he is alive to the guilt implicit in the theft and persisting thereafter. John Crowe Ransom is more responsive to the guilt than to the attribute: according to his interpretation in *God without Thunder*, the Promethean fire is science, the modern enemy, the promise of a purely secular economy opposed to religion and therefore to poetry. The gift of knowledge gave men new interests, and turned them away from veneration and worship; it brought men off their knees, and made them busy with secular concerns, eventually to be called Science. Ransom rebukes the scientists for laying rude hands upon the world, using the natural forms as grist for their mills. Science is no respecter of persons or of things, and the poet speaks of it as a modern devotee of the symbolic imagination would speak of positivism or behaviorism. I am surprised that Ransom did not force the issue to the point of asking: when Prometheus stole the

---

[1] C. Kerenyi, *Prometheus: Archetypal Image of Human Existence,* tr. Ralph Manheim. London. Thames and Hudson, 1963, p. 78.

[2] Coleridge, *Miscellanies, Aesthetic and Literary,* collected by T. Ashe. London, 1885, pp. 53–83.

fire and gave it to men, had he in mind giving them the means of becoming gods or demigods, or merely the means of survival and a chance to develop a few secular potentialities, within finite limits? When Satan offered the fruit to Eve, he promised her that it would place her among the gods: 'Taste this, and be henceforth among the gods / Thy self a goddess, not to earth confined.' (V.77–8.) Prometheus might have spoken thus to men. The promise is not entirely fraudulent: in her dream, Eve tastes the fruit and immediately flies to the clouds, where she sees the world in absolute perspective:

> Forthwith up to the clouds
> With him I flew, and underneath beheld
> The earth outstretched immense, a prospect wide
> And various.   (V.86–9.)

The common name of this vision is inspiration, with an implication that it transcends human knowledge and prediction. Milton invokes it in the Latin poems and elsewhere, associating it with the holy traces of Prometheus's fire, *Sancta Prometheae retinens vestigia flammae*, and in his prolusion on the theme that men are made happier by knowledge than by ignorance he speaks of 'that retreat of Prometheus under the leadership of Mercury into the deepest solitudes of Mount Caucasus, where he became the wisest of gods and men, insomuch that Jupiter himself is said to have asked his advice about the nuptials of Thetis'.[1] The poet of *Paradise Lost* is bound to concern himself with such themes: the cost of knowledge, the nature of poetic inspiration, the no-man's-land between earth and heaven, earth and hell, Promethean fire.

He is also concerned with the nature of deity, the Christian version of Zeus. Zeus does not appear in person in *Prometheus Bound*, he is represented there by Power and Force, and he is often denounced as a cruel god, arbitrary and tyrannical. Prometheus's complaints against him are endorsed by Hephaestus and the Chorus, so they must be taken seriously, though it is probably true that in Aeschylus Zeus never punishes the innocent. Prometheus makes the same accusation against him that Adam makes, less stridently,

---

[1] Milton, *Works*, Columbia edition, Vol. I, p. 270, and Vol. XII, p. 249.

n Book X: 'Inexplicable / Thy justice seems.' (X. 754–
this means not that God's actions are inexplicable but
parading themselves as justice is inexplicable, if justice
at a man using the word thinks it means:

> Will he draw out,
> For anger's sake, finite to infinite
> In punished man, to satisfy his rigour
> Satisfied never.   (X.803–4.)

On the other hand the relation between Prometheus and Zeus is much more dynamic than that between Adam and God the Father: the 'distance' between Adam and God is absolute, while Prometheus and Zeus are nearer kin, if not quite two of a kind. The point is that if Prometheus is to be Promethean, Zeus must be an arbitrary god, a proper object either of obedience or of revolt. There is a passage in *Estrangement* where Yeats speaks of rewriting his early story 'The Adoration of the Magi': 'I see clearly that when I rewrite "The Adoration of the Magi" the message given to the old men must be a series of seemingly arbitrary commands: A year of silence, certain rules of diet, and so on. Without the arbitrary there cannot be religion, because there cannot be the last sacrifice, that of the spirit.'[1] Prometheus refused the last sacrifice, and that is the meaning of his revolt. He thought Zeus's design upon mankind an arbitrary programme, and he identified himself with the human rather than the divine idea of justice by giving men what Zeus withheld. He refused the sacrifice of his spirit, because he identified that spirit with the human sense of justice. So he made himself available to us, like a secret agent, a traitor to his own country. This tells us something of *Paradise Lost*. Those who insist upon a liberal-democratic reading of the poem are outraged by God the Father, his cruelty, his pedantic notions of freedom and justice; heads-I-win, tails-you-lose. But Yeats is right: without the arbitrary there cannot be religion; or at least there cannot be religion as distinct from the prompting of our own

---

[1] W. B. Yeats, *Autobiographies*. London, Macmillan, 1961, p. 466.

sensibility. There can only be religion which accommodates itself to our desires. There is merit in obeying a just command, but it is not the same merit as that of obeying an unjust command: the one is a matter of genial relationships, the other is the last sacrifice. I believe because it is impossible, I obey without question. Those who go out of their way to make a case for God in *Paradise Lost* by somehow squaring his acts with the human idea of fair play are misguided, because the laws of fair dealing do not apply. The desire to make God just and reasonable in human terms is merely the desire to have him respect our common law. But God's law is statute law, arbitrary by definition. Prometheus knows this, but he refuses the last sacrifice: his sense of fair play is outraged by the sight of harassed men, and he is carried beyond himself into identification with humanity, like a modern hero stealing the Pentagon Papers. It is therefore a valid question to ask, when reading *Paradise Lost*, how much of Milton's feeling adheres to the Old Testament of Zeus, and how much to the New Testament of Prometheus and Christ. In fact, Milton had an acute sense of the arbitrary in religion. As he says in the *De Doctrina* of God's instruction about the apple: 'It was necessary that something should be forbidden or commanded as a test of fidelity, and that an act in its nature indifferent, in order that man's obedience might thereby be manifested' (Ch.X). It is worth mentioning, incidentally, that Satan doesn't begin talking like a modern liberal until he starts tempting Eve, using language congenial to her rather than to him. But there is no precise method of estimating, in Milton's poem, the rival elements in his feeling: in some respects he is the most modern of moderns, demanding that God will act with our sense of reason and justice; in other respects he yields his will to the arbitrary will of God. It is enough if we recognize that the relation between God and man is not that of I to Thou: it is, in the poem, a sterner relation, founded on authority and the demand of absolute obedience. God is the God of Thunder.

Perhaps we can move a little closer toward this idiom by recalling our sense of Greek tragedy and particularly our sense of Aeschylus. Hugh Lloyd-Jones has quoted, in *The Justice of Zeus*, two passages which testify to that stringent relation between man and God, or rather between men and gods, which I have mentioned. The first is in the *Agamemnon*, where the Chorus (lines 180f.) says that Zeus has ordained that wisdom comes by suffering: 'But even as trouble, bringing memory of pain, drops upon the mind in sleep, so wisdom comes to men despite themselves. There is a grace that comes by violence from the divine powers seated upon their awful thrones.' The second passage is in the *Eumenides* (lines 517f.) where the Chorus says, 'there are times when what is fearful is good and must remain seated to watch over men's minds: it is to men's advantage to learn good sense by constraint'.[1] I presume that the aesthetic response to those times is what we call the Sublime, when we are struck by a sudden impression of extraordinary force at large, and our response is awe or dread. I am suggesting that in reading *Paradise Lost* we should enliven the impression, largely defined in Aeschylean tragedy, that 'men are the creation only of a minor god, and have only a minor status in the universe and a minor place in the attention of the gods'.[2] We should assume that the gods are likely to deal with us as Homer's Apollo dealt with the walls of the Achaeans in the *Iliad*, throwing them down, Homer says (XV.361f.) as a boy at the seaside, when he has made a sand-castle, knocks it down again for fun. Or we should enliven the other bothersome question about the plurality of worlds, a Copernican nicety. If any of the other planets are inhabited, their inhabitants cannot be members of the one true Church or look to Christ as their Redeemer, so it is intolerably arrogant of men to think themselves of supreme concern to God. William Empson has brought up the question again as bearing upon Donne, but it is just as lively in regard to *Paradise Lost*. We can hardly stay very long with such a low estimate of the place we occupy in the universal scale of things, but we should at least admit the thought, as a qualification upon our grander idea of ourselves; as *Paradise Lost* does. We ought to read the poem with this sense in mind,

---

[1] Lloyd-Jones, *supra*, pp. 87, 92: the translation has been slightly modified in the light of the Loeb edition, translator H. Weir Smyth, editor Hugh Lloyd-Jones.
[2] Lloyd-Jones, *supra*, p. 160.

even if the effort appears perverse, because otherwise we are bound to read it as modern democrats for whom the mere history of mankind is the beginning and the end of everything. When we speak of justice, we cannot help meaning the human concept; we cannot construe a divine justice consistent with the operation of undeserved suffering in the world. This is why the plays of Aeschylus and the *City of God* of Augustine are among the most suitable prologomena to *Paradise Lost*. Readers of *Paradise Lost* who start with liberal suppositions are bound to be outraged by evidence of an arbitrary God. I would prefer to keep those suppositions in suspense and to begin with a sense of human history as possibly no more than a footnote to the divine text; even if such a sense cannot survive intact to the end. This does not mean that we make ourselves humble readers; like the poem itself, our experience of reading it is bound to contain outrage, singularity, and abuse, as well as joy and luxury. I would read the poem in a spirit comparable to that of Sri Ramakrishna who, when asked why an omnipotent God permits the operation of evil in the world, answered: 'in order to thicken the plot'.

I am implying that Milton's feeling for these matters is complicated. Perhaps the double allegiance constitutes his eagle: I have in mind a passage in the *Prometheus Misbound* of Gide in which the eagle is identified with man's conscience. Everyone should have an eagle. One of Gide's characters says, 'I do not love Man. I love what devours him. Now, what devours Man? – His eagle'.[1] Gide would have us devour our eagles, lest they devour us: if there is an equivalent motive in Milton, it is his sense of pleasure, his voluptuous recognitions. The eagle is his conscientiousness, his double allegiance. The night heals him, the day opens the wound again. If a definitive position is sought, he is neither of the devil's party nor of God's party, but drawn to division. That is why it is wrong to translate him into local terms. Christopher Caudwell has a passage in *Romance and Realism* where he links

---

[1] Gide, *Marshlands and Prometheus Misbound*, tr. George D. Painter. London. Secker and Warburg, 1953, p. 136.

the revolt of the angels, the civil war in Heaven, with another civil war nearer home. The reason why Milton's imagination allowed Satan to run away with *Paradise Lost*, he says, is that Milton's God is the foolish, arbitrary Stuart, and Satan the noble and reasonable bourgeois revolutionary. In *Paradise Regained* Milton as Christ is offered all the glitter of the Stuart Court, and rejects it: in *Samson Agonistes* he pulls down the pillars on an insolent Court that mocks him.[1] But this is too simple, it does not allow for Milton's own arbitrariness, and the complex determination of his language.

There is also a curious ambivalence in the relation between Prometheus, Satan, and Christ. Kenneth Burke has remarked that 'the Greek Lucifer had brought to man a part of divinity, but had brought it *divisively*, as an offence against the gods'. This is true, even though Prometheus's motive is good, from the human standpoint. Satan also brought to man a part of divinity, the promise of divine knowledge, though his motive was impure. In Christianity, as Burke says, 'Christ had become revised as an unambiguously benign Lucifer, bringing light as a *representative* of the Godhead'. In Prometheus and Satan the divine part is torn away from the whole, and the act is sacrilege: in Christ, it is 'integral with its source', and the act is redemptive. 'Milton's rebellious angel, in his tendency to become a hero, moves us back into the original ambiguity, where the part fluctuates between its dialectical poles as associate and dissociate of the whole.'[2] I think the fluctuation is caused by our ambivalent sense of the hero as such, our feeling about all heroes that while we try to judge them by our values, they set up their own, making our values largely irrelevant. We represent this aspect of Satan by saying that he is self-evident.

There is also in Milton an ambivalent sense of knowledge, one aspect of the 'paradox of the fortunate fall'. In *Areopagitica* and the

---

[1] Christopher Caudwell, *Romance and Realism*, ed. Samuel Hynes. Princeton. Princeton University Press, 1970, p. 48.
[2] Kenneth Burke, *The Philosophy of Literary Form*, Baton Rouge. Louisiana State University Press, second edition, 1967, pp. 59–60.

De Doctrina he says that the tree of the knowledge of good and evil was so called because 'since Adam tasted it, we not only know evil, but we know good only by means of evil'.[1] The general feeling is that knowledge is dearly bought, but finally worth the cost. 'Can it be sin to know, / Can it be death?', Satan asks. The first sign of trouble in the Garden is Eve's questioning Adam about the stars. Adam has to give a long, complicated answer, not entirely convincing, and Milton puts an end to the interrogation by telling them to seek 'No happier state, and know to know no more'. (IV.775.) The real joy of Eden before the Fall consisted in the fact that it was not necessary to question or to answer, it was sufficient to be, and to enjoy being. In Book VIII Raphael tells Adam that he should confine his questions to ordinary matters and keep away from things 'obscure and subtle'. The standard comparison is of knowledge and food, good things in moderation but not in excess. And yet the question of knowledge itself is never finally settled. When Satan says that God's ban on knowledge is suspicious, most readers agree, at least until they remind themselves of God's arbitrary will.

Again, we recognize our ambivalence in relation to power, especially when it comes to the point of obliterating our sense of ethical distinction. We have only to read Blake's 'The Tyger' or Marvell's 'Horatian Ode' to renew our feeling for the unquestionable nature of power, regardless of right and wrong, our feeling that power constitutes, in cases where it is sufficiently active, the only applicable law. Power gives its manifestations irrefutable authority, detaching them from ethical scrutiny as if they were acts of fate: it moves the actions into a theatre of spectacle, force, and destiny where the question of right and wrong is overwhelmed by the inescapable presence of power. Presence cannot be questioned by ethical considerations, it does not account for itself to anyone. Milton's description of Satan invading the Garden in Book IV responds to this sense of power detaching its possessor from the ordinary considerations of good and evil. Ithuriel and Zephon find Satan 'close at the ear of Eve': at various points in the

---

[1] Milton, *Works*, XV. 115.

poem, Satan is compared to wolves, thieves, cormorants, serpents; these are standard comparisons, but now, a few lines after calling him a toad, Milton compares him to 'a proud steed reined' (IV.858) and thereafter to the Titan Atlas (IV.987). The normal answer to this is that if we wait a while we find Milton bringing Satan low again, sending him scurrying from the Garden in the last lines of Book IV. The poet seems to be taking away with one hand what he has given with the other.

Some such account of the poem is inescapable. *Paradise Lost* is a story told for the second time: the first was in *Genesis*. But it is recited now in different circumstances. The *Genesis* story is relatively simple and direct, because it assumes an order of events within which such a story can be given, transparently. But Milton is asserting eternal Providence, and the necessity of assertion is the first sign that he, too, has lost a paradise. The paradise lost to him is a condition in which words were sanctioned by divine authority, by Revelation. Each word was finite, but language itself was transcendent, its syntax verified by God, the Logos to whom each word referred. The first mark of Milton's style is the necessity under which it labours, the necessity of asserting what once had only to be sung. If his style is problematic, the reason is that he must take upon himself the burden of enforcing meaning, he cannot merely celebrate it. So we have two factors: Milton's sense of strain and necessity; and then, immediately, his pride in the feeling that he alone is fit to assume such a burden. He cannot rely upon the continuity of shared feeling implicit in a vernacular speech, he must certify a form of speech which registers his personal responsibility for the narrative. He is writing, like every modern poet, after the Fall, and his first problem is his own sophistication, he is corrupt where he needs to be pure. By comparison with *Genesis, Paradise Lost* is opaque, clouded by necessity, obstinate where the original is free.

The question comes back to the tree of the knowledge of good and evil: 'we know good only by means of evil'. Milton is insecurely but heroically placed between freedom and necessity; the freedom of belief, the necessity of asserting belief: or, in another version, the freedom of absolute belief in God, and the necessity of reconciling God's power with human justice. The problem can only be resolved, if resolved at all, by narrative: at any chosen moment, it is insoluble or at best unsolved, it cannot be solved until the end. If we know good only by means of evil, we have to go through evil to achieve good: Milton's narrative is his way of going through. The answer to every local problem of interpretation in *Paradise Lost* is therefore: wait. Nothing is clear at the time because nothing is complete: if human justice is acknowledged at all, it is only in retrospect, when all accommodations are made. A reader who comes to the speeches of Satan, Moloch, Belial, and Mammon in Book II, for instance, will distinguish between one attitude and another, but he is likely to respond to the continuity of anger and outrage directed against a God who, in that immediate perspective, has little to recommend Him but His omnipotence. Such a reader receives Moloch's speech as mere huffing and puffing, but only if he is satisfied to let the hidden God win the war by winning this one battle. Milton curbs our sympathy for Moloch by inserting a sharp editorial, putting him in his place, but he has already let the reader go a good distance to meet the speaker. It is as though Milton's own resentment were to be expressed and then formally withdrawn. He does the same with Belial, gives him his head, then pulls him down. The difference in that case is that he writes the editorial first, tells us that Belial is a smart rhetorician, and then lets him speak. The rhythm of the entire poem begins to assert itself as 'no' followed by 'yes'; revolt admonished at last by obedience. In the nature of the case, the revolt is likely to be the more stirring part, a call to arms, and modern readers have responded to it in that spirit, they hardly take the obedience as more than a formal gesture. But the question is difficult, and it was not settled by Blake or Shelley, who found Milton's true spirit in the revolt, and little or nothing of it in the obedience. Stevens spoke of 'the yes of the realist spoken because he must / Say yes, spoken because under every no / Lay a passion for yes that had never been broken'.[1] It is a hard question to decide, in Milton's case, which is the greater passion, the immediate no or the final yes. He

---

[1] Stevens, *Collected Poems*, p. 320.

can only deal with his motives extensively, not resolving them at any moment but letting them range, narratively, affronting one another, until the end. To use Kenneth Burke's distinction, it is like the difference between a chord and an arpeggio using the same notes: the chord brings all the notes together, with whatever violence, simultaneously, and the violence demands to be resolved, if it is extreme: the arpeggio uses the same notes, but extensively, in latitude and narrative, and the meaning is the entire sequence, as if heard a second time. The harsh notes are then grace notes, piquant in passing. The great merit of narrative is that there will be time enough for everything, the truth is declared only when all the evidence is in. So we postpone its anatomy. The best reader of *Paradise Lost* is the one who is most patient, most prepared to hold judgment in abeyance. If a detail or an episode seems disproportionate, he is willing to wait, to see how it looks at the end of the day. This applies in detail to our reading of Milton's verse, the answer is never given in the line or the phrase, but only at length in the verse paragraph, the book, the poem. Milton's narrative calls for a patient reader not because the poem is long but because common judgments are importunate. But the Yahwist of *Genesis* is a different kind of narrator, he is continuously at one with his story, convinced not only that it is true, and true at any chosen moment, but that it is the paradigm of all truth. The rhythm of yes and no is alien to him, because his testimony to the truth of his story is constant, his will is never distinguishable from the movement of the narrative. Milton's relation to the story is tendentious, and even if his orthodoxy could be established in the end, it could not be shown to have kept him identified with the story, moment by moment. So far as the story demands to be believed, that is, as a strict account of the history of mankind, it insists upon the question of truth and falsehood, knowledge and ignorance, and Milton deals with it on those terms. If the poem ever strikes the reader as harsh, it is because Milton found the question of truth incorrigible. No wonder he resorted to a different idiom whenever he could: notably to the idiom of pleasure, as in the Garden, 'the sweet of life', as Adam calls it in Book VII; or the equivalent of that sweet, the joy of God's creation, the elation with which the new world of natural forms is described in Book VII. The creation of the fishes, for instance, is described in terms of feminine beauty and luxuriance:

> . . . part single or with mate
> Graze the sea weed their pasture, and through groves
> Of coral stray, or sporting with quick glance
> Show to the sun their waved coats dropped with gold. (VII.403–6).

Nevertheless, Milton cannot be continuously at one with his story, he proceeds by giving and taking away; he makes difficulties for himself, because his will insists upon them, and then he lives to surmount them. The relation between his imagination and its chosen material is a contentious relation, but we have some reason to think he would not have had it otherwise. I think he supposed that his God would come in thunder.

In general, I assume that a writer's happiest occasions, unless he is an inveterate Promethean, are those in which he feels that he is merely transcribing reality, and that in the transcription his imaginative desires are fulfilled. He is happy if he feels that the natural appearance of things contains and, at the first polite invitation, discloses not only Nature's being but its meaning and value. At such a time, it is possible to lay aside the old quarrel of subject and object, fact and value, imagination and reality. Hofmannsthal records a magical occasion of that kind in the Chandos letter, where he speaks of understanding the whole of existence as one great unit in which the spiritual and the physical elements were at peace together, Nature was equally embodied in all its manifestations, and, he says, 'in all expressions of Nature I felt myself'. The writer is content to write, at such a time, to transcribe the given, without more ado than transcription requires. He does not fear that perception is an optical illusion. He willingly acts as secretary to Nature, taking dictation without fuss or interrogation. Adam naming the beasts is the paradigm of this felicity, since he is present in the naming, the words. The theory of poetic inspiration is charming because it ministers to that desire, it puts aside aesthetic or moral questions in the assumption of an unquestionable source.

A poet would be happy to transcribe if he were convinced that transcription is enough, that what he transcribes is the truth of things, including his own truth. In a secular age, theories of inspiration become theories of imagination, because the source is deemed to be man himself. Imagination is the secular equivalent of God as creator, including especially God as self-creator, in Coleridge's phrase 'the infinite I AM'. Theology becomes aesthetics: hence our questions about the nature of the imagination, and its relation to the activity of the senses. These questions are contentious because we feel that if they were pushed back a little or pressed to the limit they would touch upon fundamental issues inseparable from the question of God and man. We might wish to keep such an enquiry within decent bounds, but we feel that a searching analysis would disclose incorrigible questions of life and death. Officially, we say that we are discussing the relation between a poet's imagination and his chosen or fated materials, but unofficially we know that we are arguing about truth and error, knowledge and ignorance, corruption and innocence.

But the question of Milton's imagination and its relation to the loss of paradise is a special question in one respect. There is a passage in Coleridge where the theme is the relation between the senses and the imagination: Coleridge is speaking of the 'despotism of the eye', the degree to which that one sensory power enforces itself over and beyond its fellows, even to the extent of putting the imagination at risk. And he says that 'we are restless because invisible things are not the objects of vision'. It is easy to understand that Milton's imagination is especially restless, since hardly anything in the materials of *Paradise Lost* is an object of vision. Many of the disputed parts of the poem arise from this predicament, that Milton is forcing invisible things to act as if they were visible. Bachelard has commented severely on that passage in the first Book of *Paradise Lost* where Milton describing the ejection of Satan and his companions from Heaven tells us that their fall took 'nine times the space that measures day and night / To mortal men'. (I.50–51.) Satan is the symbol of moral fall, Bachelard says, 'but when Milton presents the fallen angel as an object hustled and thrown out of heaven, he puts out the light of the symbol'.[1] The short answer to this is that there is no special language for invisible things, and a poet must do what he can: he cannot avoid writing of them as if they were visible, and of metaphysical things as if they were physical. He depends upon the resources of analogy and metaphor to suggest those things for which there are no given names. In the particular case, Milton would claim that he was merely following the old description of the fall of the Titans in Hesiod's *Theogony*. Or he might claim that he had done well to compound a language for space and time simultaneously, and that the words complained of are more than a longwinded way of saying 'nine days'. Bachelard would not be assuaged by these considerations. He maintains that the only convincing way of treating the problem would be by somehow presenting the fall through all the senses simultaneously. The fall should be, he says, metaphor and reality at the same time. Perhaps he has in mind the more diverse account of the fall of the angels in the *Confessions* of St. Augustine (XIII.viii). In principle, there is no valid argument against recourse to analogy and metaphor when it is a question of invoking what lies beyond the senses: one can only question particular instances which depend upon a relation between image and idea, or between the universal and its concrete embodiment.

I have remarked that Milton cannot always be at one with his story, and now that he is restless because invisible things are not the objects of vision but must somehow be represented in terms of vision. These factors brought together point to a certain predicament and to a corresponding propensity of the imagination. If such an imagination cannot have an easy fellowship with its materials, it cannot be on easy terms with Nature. There is bound to be a feeling that Nature does not mean enough, or that it is sluggish in sustaining the grandest intimations. An act will not be deemed valid because it issues from Nature, but because it issues from one's own sensibility. In a quarrel between mind and Nature it is possible to take either side; the mind engaged in the

---

[1] Gaston Bachelard, *L'Air et les songes*. Paris. Corti, 1943, pp. 109–110. (My translation.)

quarrel may choose to lay aside the dispute and acknowledge Nature as first and last source. There are imaginations of this kind, like Herbert's, they take their bearings from the world of natural forms, and suppose a teleology at work in sensory evidence. But Milton's imagination is not willing to lay aside the quarrel, it does not ground its values upon assumptions of order or purpose in Nature, but rather upon a sense of its own power. Milton's imagination is indeed an imagination of belief, I see no real difficulty in calling it a Christian imagination, but its deepest conviction is lavished upon its own power: the problem then is to bring other beliefs into harmony with the original belief, the imagination's felt relation to itself. The relation between Milton's imagination and its chosen objects is peremptory, it takes what it needs, and subdues resistant things to its nature. In the presence of this imagination we think again of the question of power and the question of value; such an imagination is likely to work by *fiat* upon its materials. It is natural for us to think of it in terms of action rather than of knowledge, and among theorists of the imagination Sartre has encouraged us to think of imagination as an act of consciousness. If we think of imagination in this way we free ourselves from the habit of thinking of images as little pictures in the mind: images are registered as acts of the mind, their content is their nature as acts, their force and direction. The Promethean imagination is in a special sense an act of the mind, because it seizes what it requires, it steals the divine fire. We are justified in finding such an imagination in Milton because of the impression of force and restlessness in his language, the sense of a grace of style that comes by violence; and the corresponding impression of force and restlessness in his relation to natural forms. In the relation between the imagination and Nature Milton sets up conditions so favourable to the imagination that Nature can defend itself only by calling upon the stubbornness of matter. Reading Milton, we find it necessary to remind ourselves that there are other poets, and that his *Paradise Lost* is surrounded by a space on all sides occupied either by nothing or by entirely different sounds; such is the poem's power to make over the entire world in its spirit. This is presumably what Empson had in mind by calling Milton 'an absolutist, an all-or-none man': 'All else is unimportant beside one thing, he is continually deciding; he delights in the harshness of a theme which makes all human history turn on an absolutely trivial action.'[1] I would say 'absolutely arbitrary', but it makes little difference, Milton's imagination delights in driving things, including his own imagination, to the limit. He would not be willing to commit the ordinary sins, but only those in which a direct affront to God's authority is declared: blasphemy, pride, presumption. The Promethean imagination is more deeply responsive to harsh themes than to genial themes, to the arbitrary than to the reasonable; it does not delight in the continuity of reasons, causes, effects, mediations between the one hand and the other. It delights rather in an act of the will, without any further ground in the nature of the case. Yeats describes rhetoric as 'the will trying to do the work of the imagination'. In Milton, there is a remarkably close liaison between will and imagination; so much so that it is often hard to tell the difference between them. They are merged in the act, though separable in theory. The meaning of things must be brought into relation with the temper of the imagination, and this is bound to be a difficult relation. It is difficult because Milton expects the world to be like his own demanding imagination: the world as it is imagined is required to resemble the imagination which construes it, and perhaps it is bound to do so. If we begin with the imagination, we proceed to realize the world in terms of that imagination rather than any other; we are tracking down the logic of an imagination. This is only another way of saying that Prometheus's most vigorous relation is to himself; and the next vigorous is his relation to Zeus. Prometheus is self-conscious, conscious of himself as a hero, and he is conscious of the line of force which joins him to Zeus. The other characters in Aeschylus's play, Hephaestus, Power, Force, and the rest, are mediating characters through whom Prometheus conducts his quarrel with Zeus. He needs Zeus, if for no other reason than that he needs a force at least equal and opposite and preferably greater than himself. He needs in Zeus a

---

[1] William Empson, *The Structure of Complex Words*. London. Chatto and Windus, 1952, p. 101.

force sharing many of the same qualities of imagination, but more powerful and more arbitrary. These mighty opposites meet on the intervening ground, and at last they join together. So the Promethean imagination in poetry has a sense of the world as similarly constituted: the world is likely to appear harsh, arbitrary, and intractable, if it is to answer the strange imagination which construes it in that spirit. The imagination imagines itself, and seeks for this purpose commensurate materials. It cannot be satisfied by the apparitions which satisfy other people; apparitions, for example, of justice operant in the affairs of the world, or of common people cheerfully engaged in common interests. These evidences are likely to disgust the Promethean imagination because of the banality of their satisfactions. I think it significant and appropriate that when John Crowe Ransom admonished his readers to restore to God His thunder, he was just then meditating, as a literary critic, upon Milton's *Paradise Lost*. Ransom is a man of peace, but he felt and was right to feel that we should not turn the grand story of human life and death into a bourgeois consolation prize; we should not proceed as though everything were explicable in our terms. It would not be good if those things which affront us were to be removed. I am sure that Milton has a good deal of this feeling, mixed with feeling of a more easygoing, liberal kind.

As an example of Milton's hauteur in dealing with his material, I quote the temptation of Eve in Book IX (lines 664f.):

> She scarce had said, though brief, when now more bold
> The tempter, but with show of zeal and love
> To man, and indignation at his wrong,
> New part puts on, and as to passion moved,
> Fluctuates disturbed, yet comely and in act
> Raised, as of some great matter to begin.

This may sound like Milton's editorial, warning us against Satan's bogus rhetoric, but in fact it is a neutral presentation: the show of zeal and love need not yet be insincere, the new part need not be false. There is as yet nothing to prevent us from taking the verb 'puts on' in the respectable sense, as in Tindale's 'Ye have put off the old man with his works, and have put on the new'. This sense of the verb had to be retained to allow for cases of repentance. Milton has it in the *Eikonoclastes* (VI.9), 'Putting off the courtier, he now puts on the philosopher'. (OED 45 d.(b).) And the next passage shows Satan for the moment in an entirely reputable light:

> As when of old some orator renowned
> In Athens or free Rome, where eloquence
> Flourished, since mute, to some great cause addressed,
> Stood in himself collected, while each part,
> Motion, each act won audience ere the tongue,
> Sometimes in highth began, as no delay
> Of preface brooking through his zeal of right.
> So standing, moving, or to highth upgrown
> The tempter all impassioned thus began.

Again, Satan is the Roman orator, centrally placed in a tradition of political rhetoric guaranteed by Cicero and Quintilian, eloquence at the service of gravity. That reference to 'free Rome' echoes through the whole passage, amplified by the 'zeal of right': we are given no cause to think either phrase ironic. Satan is a Roman with a case on his hands which we are not obliged, at this moment, to think a bad one: it could turn out to be good, or at least we are allowed to wait upon that charity. In fact, it turns out to be a complicated piece of casuistry, but its rhetorical corruption does not become clear until quite late in its progress, and the speech is never allowed to fall below a certain level of respectability, since it must be good enough to convince Eve, who is no fool. It is no answer to say that Eve wants to be misled, and that even bad arguments are good enough to convince someone who wants to be convinced. The casuistry is not crass:

> O sacred, wise, and wisdom-giving plant,
> Mother of science, now I feel thy power
> Within me clear, not only to discern
> Things in their causes, but to trace the ways
> Of highest agents, deemed however wise.
> Queen of this universe, do not believe
> Those rigid threats of death; ye shall not die:
> How should ye? By the fruit? It gives you life

> To knowledge. By the threatener? Look on me,
> Me who have touched and tasted, yet both live,
> And life more perfect have attained than fate
> Meant me, by venturing higher than my lot.

The association between Mother of Science and Queen of the Universe has the effect of identifying Eve with the divine power concealed in the tree. The pliancy of the argument is set off against the rigidity of God's command. Most of the effect comes from Satan's being at once questioner and answerer, he is willing to raise with himself the difficulties which a prosecuting lawyer would raise in a trial. This makes him sound at least more open-minded than God, and it allows him to use with Eve the idiom of courage and daring: instead of commands to be obeyed, she hears now of risks to be taken, courage against inertia. Empson has argued that the appeal which does the trick is in these lines:

> Or will God incense his ire
> For such a petty trespass, and not praise
> Rather your dauntless virtue, whom the pain
> Of death denounced, whatever thing death be,
> Deterred not from achieving what might lead
> To happier life, knowledge of good and evil.

Satan is speaking as if Eve had already eaten the apple. God will be so impressed and edified by her courage that he will ignore the technical sin of disobedience: maybe He wants her to eat the apple, thereby showing that the letter killeth, the spirit giveth life, and most particularly the spirit of heroic risk and courage. 'Deterred not from achieving what might lead to happier life': I emphasize 'might' here, with its suggestion that Eve should go ahead even if the power of the apple were doubtful rather than certain, since it takes more courage to bet everything on an outside chance. Milton is giving Satan the kind of arguments which he himself would use in a pamphlet, with only a slight twist here and there, if he were arguing the cause of freedom and responsibility. They are both antique Romans and the excitement of the passage arises from the presence of an even greater casuist than Satan, audible between the lines, ostensibly in the role of narrator.

It is in this sense that the Milton of *Paradise Lost* is a Promethean imagination. He is never willing to let those things speak for themselves which declare themselves as facts. His will has made of his imagination a hero. There is a passage in Ortega's meditation on 'the hero' where he says of Homer's characters that they 'belong to the same world as their desires'; that is, they are not heroes. A hero is one whose desires belong to another world than the one he inhabits, and often that other world is attested by those desires and by nothing else at all producible. Every movement the hero makes must first 'overcome custom and invent a new kind of gesture.'[1] Prometheus is such a gesture. His desires as a demigod turn his actions toward man and the earth: he might have lived among his own kind without striking such a gesture. The Promethean imagination is never completely at home to itself in its own place: always restless, it insists on transfiguring the given world until a new world rises fulfilling the passion which produced it. Nothing is more real to such an imagination than its relation to the exercise of will; unless we give equal allowance, as we must, to every force in the given world which offers resistance. The imagination counts upon that resistance, it does not sue for peace. We register this by saying that Milton invests at least as much feeling in justifying his imagination to himself as in justifying the ways of God to men. His imagination is as demanding as the God it encounters.

I have been emphasizing the Promethean motive in Milton's imagination. This is not the same as the Satanic motive which most readers acknowledge as predominant in the first books of *Paradise Lost*. Prometheus persists, as a quality of Milton's imagination, even when Satan has been reduced to a relatively minor role in the play. But I do not assert that the Promethean motive is the only emphasis one has to make, in giving a fair account of the poem. Milton's art is so comprehensive that any approach to it, consistently pursued, is bound to be misleading. I confess I have more serious misgivings about a Promethean reading of Milton than of any of the other writers discussed in these lectures. To be

---

[1] José Ortega y Gasset, *Meditations on Quixote*, trs. Evelyn Rugg and Diego Marin. New York. Norton, 1961, pp. 140–1.

somewhat more specific: what my account of the poem has not adequately emphasized is the joy of the language, and the credences given in that joy, the sense in which *Paradise Lost* invites the response of comparing it with, say, Haydn's *Creation*. Again, my account has not sufficiently acknowledged the dramatic power of the Son; or the radiance of Eve. Comparison of Eve with Pandora is misleading, though justified so far as it goes, because Pandora is merely the luxurious punishment for another's crime, and Eve is the crime itself and the form of its desperate glory. Eve is the opulence of the poem, her aura surrounds the verse even when the ostensible theme is something else: 'Show to the sun their waved coats dropped with gold'; fishes, but feminine, richly on show, under the sign of Eve. Again, the Promethean reading of *Paradise Lost* helps us to register the relation between God and Satan, but it leaves the Son too much in shadow, the Father's shadow, it does not take the full force of the Son as Redeemer. The Promethean motive, I should remark, does not prescribe the content of a writer's mind, but rather its dominant capacity, a predilection of form or tone, a characteristic disposition of the mind when engaged with any experience. The name marks a vocation of consciousness, and it leads the reader to expect in the writer a corresponding choice among the available modes of experience, even if the definitive choice is a plague on all their houses. In the case of *Paradise Lost* the passages I have not underlined are those in which the demands of the Promethean imagination are held in suspense, and Milton lavishes his talent upon the plenitude of what is merely given: the Woman, the Garden, the Son.

The Peremptory
Imagination

ACCORDING to the myth of Prometheus, men are receivers of stolen goods and therefore almost as guilty as the thief. The effect of the theft is that we are enabled to differentiate ourselves from nature, much to our advantage, but the advantage is acquired at the price of guilt and division. The Chorus in Shelley's *Prometheus Unbound* tells the hero that as a result of his theft of knowledge there was kindled in man

> a thirst which outran
> Those perishing waters; a thirst of fierce fever,
> Hope, love, doubt, desire, which consume him for ever.[1]

Minds as diverse as Vitruvius, Rousseau, and Lévi-Strauss like to imagine a time when there was virtually no distinction between men and nature; animals and men alike lived on earth in the freedom of body, ate raw food, and enjoyed the elements. Derrida speaks, in *De la grammatologie*, of 'la complicité qui lie pacifiquement la bonne société à soi-même dans son jeu'. But there came a day when men felt a desire to rise above their station, distinguishing themselves from animals and the things of earth, as if to move from vocative speech to written text. No longer content with the sun's warming power, men began to cook their food with fire, refuting their dependence upon the sun and their fellowship with animals. The fire which Prometheus stole was the means by which men demanded a new destiny, and took on the guilt of achieving it. Fire enabled them to move from nature to culture, but it made culture a dangerous possession: it made tragedy probable. The Promethean fire was not originally intended for man, it was part of a divine order of things and it has always retained, in its stolen history, traces of an outraged origin. It is not fanciful to think that man by receiving the stolen fire made himself an 'abomination', a freak of nature, to be added to the list of freaks execrated in Leviticus. We have found the stolen fire identified with reason and knowledge, but it is probably better to identify it with the

---

[1] Shelley, *Selected Poetry*, edited by Neville Rogers. London. Oxford University Press, 1969, p. 77.

symbolic imagination: we have not grown so accustomed to the creative power of imagination as to think it common, in the nature of the human case, like knowledge or reason. We think imagination a wonderful power, unpredictable and diverse, and we are satisfied to call it divine and to ascribe to it an early association with transgression. A Promethean says of it that it is the most precious part of man, perhaps the only precious part, the only respect in which man's claim to superior character is tenable.

Already, certain possibilities present themselves. It is possible to feel that nature is null, a brute force of no distinction until it has been transfigured by the imagination. Or, the same feeling in other words, that nature is redeemed only when it is transformed as culture. Such an argument means that the typically human value arises from the act of imagination, which is deemed to make all the difference. This is largely Blake's position. But it is also possible to feel that a sharp distinction between nature and culture is unnecessary, since both terms partake of universal vitality and are perhaps equally signs of God's power in the world. According to that view, the natural world is 'the ground of our beseeching', and the proper function of imagination is to bring man and nature into the richest possible state of accord, to restore a lost paradise on earth. This is often Wordsworth's position, and Blake thought it a coward's charter, an ignoble treaty signed by a great poet gone soft. The idiom of harmony and reconciliation is alien to Promethean imaginations, which delight rather in tension and struggle, the exercise of will. We feel of Blake that he has transferred to his own mind the struggle between Zeus and Prometheus, naming them Urizen and Orc to prolong the battle in his own poetic character. He assumes responsibility for the war, lest a deadly peace result from inertia.

Blake and Wordsworth, Nietzsche and Wagner: the history of feeling is registered in such terms. In 1888 Nietzsche attacked Wagner for the effeminacy of his *Parsifal*. The composer had gone decadent, he said, cultivating the luxury of the senses, making the spirit morbid, appealing to our cowardice. Nietzsche was outraged by the music, its seductiveness, the incorrigible charm with which it dissolved the tensions of true experience, laying its audiences to

rest like tired children on Abraham's bosom.[1] In the Preface to
The Excursion Wordsworth wrote:

> while my voice proclaims
> How exquisitely the individual Mind
> (And the progressive powers perhaps no less
> Of the whole species) to the external World
> Is fitted: and how exquisitely, too,
> Theme this but little heard of among Men,
> The external World is fitted to the Mind;
> And the creation (by no lower name
> Can it be called) which they with blended might
> Accomplish:- This is our high argument.

But Blake wrote along the margin: 'You shall not bring me down
to believe such fitting & fitted. I know better & please your
Lordship'.[2] We cannot say that Blake knew better, but what he
knew was different, and because knowledge is personal he would
not question its report. 'I see in Wordsworth,' he says, 'the Natural
Man rising up against the Spiritual Man Continually, & then he
is No Poet but a Heathen Philosopher at Enmity against all true
Poetry or Inspiration'.[3] The natural man lives in pleromatic union
with nature, he takes his moral bearings from the natural world,
denies his own will and is therefore a liar. The spiritual man takes
as the focus of his life the soul, Blake's visionary power, the imagination, he accepts responsibility for its actions. To Blake, pleromatic
union is merely a condition in which the imagination has abdicated.

The difference between the two poets is that Blake starts from a
sense of his own imagination, and construes the given world in
that demanding light. His poems have one concern: to enact a
consequential epic of human life, starting from the imagination as

---

[1] Nietzsche, *Werke*, VI 3. Berlin. Walter de Gruyter, 1969, pp. 28, 37–8, 'Ihr
findet nirgends eine angenehmere Art, euren Geist zu entnerven, eure Männ-
lichkeit unter einem Rosengebüsche zu vergessen . . . Wie er uns damit den
Krieg macht! uns, den freien Geistern! . . . man muss beissen können, um
hier nicht anzubeten. Wohlan, alter Verführer!'
[2] Blake, *Complete Writings*, edited by Geoffrey Keynes. London. Oxford University Press, 1966, p. 784.
[3] *Ibid.*, p. 782.

the distinctively original power, the alpha of human history. Imagination is the secular manifestation of divine power; an appeal to the imagination is an appeal to that divinity which the appellant feels within himself as his creative power. To Blake, God is the God of the Old Testament, his power embodied in wrath and prophecy, his presence in the world identified now with the imperative of the human imagination. God and the imagination are one, to Blake as to Stevens. But to Wordsworth, God is a principle of affection to be acknowledged now in acts of sympathy between man and man, as between man and nature. Wordsworth starts not from a sense of his imagination as an imperative power, but from a feeling of affinity between man and the world as a sign of natural law: he then moves toward a more complete accommodation between man's spirit and the spirit he feels at large in the natural world. If it is agreed that Wordsworth's terms have their origin in human feeling rather than in the language of natural science, I see no difficulty in reconciling what has just been said with Keats's ascription, following Hazlitt, of the 'egotistical sublime' to Wordsworth. The subjective imagination is merely set off against that impartial sublime which Keats attributed to Shakespeare and to dramatic poets of his own poetical character. Wordsworth's effort is imaginative in the sense that it is concerned with making the possible actual, and since the good of man is his object the imagination is a moral possession. Wordsworth believes that the terms which apply to human feeling have their bearing, by analogy, upon the world of natural phenomena.[1] The imaginative effort to fulfil the analogy is a poet's form of prayer. Wordsworth is dedicated to the emancipation of feeling, and to the morality which depends upon that freedom, a morality of natural law more profound than any subsequent distinctions between one man and another. Hostile forces in life are those which defeat the spirit of that law. Blake, on the other hand, is dedicated to the primacy of vision, a strictly human power superhuman in its origin: he feels no loyalty to Wordsworthian recognitions and acknowledgements, since these are tokens of a law that man has not

---

[1] Cf. Jacques Monod, *Chance and Necessity*, translated by Austryn Wainhouse, New York. Knopf, 1971, p. 30.

established. Blake believes that the natural world may be redeemed by man's imagination, may be rendered human and therefore transfigured: Wordsworth believes that the natural world is already blessed, and that man has but to recognize that condition and live accordingly: such a life would mean man's redemption. Blake's most complete relation is to his own imagination, which he registers in the creation of Los; his relation to the given world is defiant, in this respect like Prometheus's relation to Zeus in Goethe's poem, where the hero is shown making men in his own image and setting them to ignore the great god. Blake does not ask his reader to insult God, but to deny the reality of any creation from which man is absent.

In Blake, the Promethean imagination is a form of energy, the 'Eternal Delight' of *The Marriage of Heaven and Hell*: to construe the world in its terms is to project that energy into the otherwise merely natural world: the result is a life of high tension and activity. Bachelard has said of Blake's words that we recognize in them 'an imagination that lives, or a life that imagines':[1] in either version, thought is a manifestation of being, created by its movement. The content of thought is activity. The nature of Blake's feeling is that it moves, and lives in movement: his characteristic syntax is that of assertion and interjection, his relation to discourse is that of the aphorism, which takes possession of a certain area of feeling and then moves forward. The words are not intended to describe or adorn something already invoked, but to announce the direction which feeling is to take. When we read, in the second Book of Blake's *Milton*, 'There is a Moment in each Day that Satan cannot find', we take the line as a call to action, an intervention. The words clear a space in the reader's mind, so that his feeling may move in that direction. So, too, we speak of Blake's visionary power, but not to denote a separation of the seeing subject from a visible object; the power has little to do with knowledge, and everything to do with desire and possession. What it desires and possesses is the freedom of its own action. This power is distinct from Reason, because Reason endorses limitation, prescribes circumference, and

---

[1] Bachelard, *L'Air et les songes*. Paris. Corti, 1943, pp. 94, 97.

turns imagination into rock and sand. Blake says of 'reasonings' in the first chapter of *Jerusalem*,

> Reasonings like vast Serpents
> Infold around my limbs, bruising my minute articulations.[1]

In the eyes of Reason, as in Blake's Tiriel, both day and night are dark, because Reason is merely 'the ratio of all we have already known' and it is limited to 'the same dull round'.[2] Like 'the Philosophy of Five Senses', Reason is merely the sum of its given conclusions, it cannot create, it cannot give life, it cannot transcend its terms: like Memory, it is trapped within its limits, its 'rotten rags' set off against the divine garment of Inspiration.[3] 'Imagination has nothing to do with Memory', Blake says, because imagination is turned toward a future consistent with its power, lavish of its own life; Memory is merely a basement of gone sensations. Those writers, like Wordsworth and Proust, who are willing to deal in memory, present it as a compact with the past which enables the perceiver to make what he can of it: by acknowledging the weight of the event, he is allowed to lift it, then to transfigure it. This is not sufficiently radical for Blake, who regards circumstances as mere fragments of nature and denies that they have any right to control the act of vision. Blake is a Promethean because he insists on hastening the process by which nature becomes culture, and he disowns the natural elements which persist. To Blake, therefore, the human question is a question of speed, of accelerating the process, too slow so long as it remains in Zeus's charge, by which man fulfills his possibilities. The mood of his imagination is therefore imperative because it is creative, the human mind is in a hurry, it exerts pressure upon feeling, through the language, to aspire toward a future consistent with the spirit of imagination. Blake's sentences are imperative even when they seem indicative, because his speech is an act of violence breaking upon the silence of inertia and habit. The words have only one object: to create a new life under their auspices, embodying a corresponding perfection. Those who merely reason see with dead eyes, the 'vegetable eyes' which Blake describes in *Milton*, they see only the hem of the garment.

---

[1] Blake, *Complete Writings*, p. 635.   [2] *Ibid.*, p. 97.   [3] *Ibid.*, p. 783.

The Peremptory Imagination

Blake celebrates the imagination as the faculty of vision, but in some respects it is an inadequate idiom: he often appears to need a complete Philosophy of the Act, in which the question of subject and object is overwhelmed by the force of gesture, movement, and action. Nature is to be rendered human, that is, felt as human, transformed to culture. Symbols are to speak for man in the world, receiving his most intimate feeling and hiding it within the symbolic object. When we say that symbols are at once subject and object, this is what we mean, but we require that they acknowledge their subject as master, in the end. In practice, there is always a gap or a void between subject and object, however idealist the official programme, and a mind of Blake's persuasion cannot help finding the ostensibly independent object a scandal, nature usurping the role of culture. The trouble is that the extreme symbolist, no matter where he turns his eyes, can never see anything as precious as his own imagination: by that imperious standard, every encounter is a disappointment, nothing actually seen lives up to the faculty by which it is seen, no mere object can have the radiance of the imagination that perceives it. Even if the natural world is registered as a forest of symbols, the symbolist is never satisfied, the forest is never dense enough or high enough to satisfy the power within. To Blake, nature is fallen, redemption is an act of vision, and if the alchemy of the Word falls back into the mere chemistry of nature, the imaginative magic must be reasserted against resistance. 'To the Eyes of the Man of Imagination', Blake writes in a letter to Dr. Trusler (August 23, 1799), 'Nature is Imagination itself'; the sentence gives every credence to the imagination, and it gives Nature only as much presence as is compatible with the primacy of the imagination, it is a secondary substance to be sublimed away. When Wordsworth wrote of the influence of natural objects as calling forth and strengthening the imagination, Blake answered: 'Natural Objects always did & now do weaken, deaden & obliterate Imagination in me'.[1] Unredeemed Nature is hateful to Blake because sullen and impervious, like a man who refuses to hear the word of God. He is in a rush to transfigure the

---

[1] *Ibid.*, p. 783.

world, and he hates those objects in nature which show themselves intractable: when he says, 'Nature is Imagination itself', we read, 'Let it be so'.

We say of naturalism in literature that it presents conditions so favourable to the mere facts of the case that it virtually nullifies the imagination. But symbolism gives an impression of the world so favourable to the imagination and so careless of the mere facts that one such fact may almost be exchanged for another, so little is its inherent character allowed to count: the object is merely yet another occasion for the subject. Yeats said of Blake that 'the limitation of his view was from the very intensity of his vision; he was a too literal realist of imagination, as others are of nature; and because he believed that the figures seen by the mind's eye, when exalted by inspiration, were "eternal existences", symbols of divine essences, he hated every grace of style that might obscure their lineaments'.[1] It can hardly be expected that the eye and the mind's eye will always have their different rights fulfilled: on most occasions, one of these instruments is dominant, at some cost to the attainment of justice. In Book XI of *The Prelude* Wordsworth says that the eye is 'the most despotic of our senses' and that it often overwhelms 'the heart'. I cannot recall any occasion on which he acknowledged that the mind's eye can defeat empiricists by seceding from phenomena, withdrawing into a sanctuary which is inhabited only by symbols of its own devising. Blake was impatient to see the work of the symbol completed, objects in nature transformed to subjects in experience. This is true as a general account. But the strength of the long prophetic books, when they are strong, is in their patience, their feeling of latitude and time, their willing sense of the imagination as a process, not necessarily a sudden revelation. I am thinking particularly of *cantabile* passages like the 'Vision of beatitude' in the first Book of *Milton*, in which natural phenomena are indeed rendered human, but not abruptly or by sleight-of-hand. In such passages, the imagination is content to wait, confident that the conversion to human terms will come in good time:

---

[1] Yeats, *Essays and Introductions*, London. Macmillan, 1961, pp. 119–120.

The Peremptory Imagination

Thou seest the gorgeous clothed Flies that dance & sport
in summer
Upon the sunny brooks & meadows: every one the dance
Knows in its intricate mazes of delight artful to weave:
Each one to sound his instruments of music in the dance,
To touch each other & recede, to cross & change & return.[1]

The source of Blake's extraordinary delicacy, in such a passage, is his recognition that 'every Natural Effect has a Spiritual Cause', and that cause and effect are in their proper sequence. The dance fulfills a Platonic form, with little or no loss in the embodiment. Blake's temperamental impatience is held in check, but the restraint is gentle, satisfied to find the feeling transpiring in the dance. It is as if he had already foreseen, in the empirical actions, their fulfilment as a dance, and were content, for once, to wait. The actions themselves aspire to the condition of form, so he need not be in a hurry, driving them ahead. There are a few passages in the prophetic poems in which Blake invokes a pastoral time when the work of imagination was already complete, as in the mind which conceived the Platonic forms: this is his paradise before the Fall. But more often he takes the Fall for granted, and the natural object is in need of redemption. When the work of redemption appears easy and the objects willing to be transformed, he lets the process run at its own pace: when the objects appear sullen, he sends out words to compel them.

Sometimes the imagination is defeated; then the mind falls back upon the senses and lies at the mercy of its sensations. Yeats spoke of a new naturalism that leaves man 'helpless before the contents of his own mind',[2] and this supposes that the imagination is null, enslaved. Blake's version of that condition is given in the sixth Night of *Vala*, where he says of the 'ruined spirits' that 'Beyond the bounds of their own self their senses cannot penetrate'.[3] This is the 'same dull round' of sensation, the tired animal in his cage; or, in the idiom of *Jerusalem*, it is the return to vegetable existence.

---

[1] Blake, *Complete Writings*, p. 512.

[2] Yeats, *Essays and Introductions*, p. 405.

[3] Blake, *Complete Writings*, p. 314.

In *Vala* when Los falls away from his imaginative task, he becomes helpless before sensation, and loses the name of action. Blake says of him, in a phrase used again in *Milton*:

> he became what he beheld:
> He became what he was doing: he was himself transform'd.[1]

This marks the defeat of perception, when the mind is captured by the sensations directed upon it by nature. At this point the blended might of man and nature is perverted: man has yielded to nature, has become a slave to natural phenomena and the resultant sensations. To Blake, the inescapable fact is that Nature, considered as separate from man, is without spirit. 'Nature Teaches nothing of Spiritual Life but only of Natural Life.'[2] Spiritual life is possessed only by the imagination: or, as Blake says in *The Marriage of Heaven and Hell*, 'Where man is not, nature is barren'.[3] Where nature is seen as rich, man is present through his imagination, but what he sees on those occasions, however wonderful, is only a glimpse of that Eternity which is the continuity of Vision. One of the most ravishing passages in Blake is such a glimpse in the second Book of *Milton*:

> the White-thorn, lovely May,
> Opens her many lovely eyes listening; the Rose still sleeps,
> None dare to wake her; soon she bursts her crimson curtain'd bed
> And comes forth in the majesty of beauty; every Flower,
> The Pink, the Jessamine, the Wall-flower, the Carnation,
> The Jonquil, the mild Lilly, opes her heavens; every Tree
> And Flower & Herb soon fill the air with an innumerable Dance,
> Yet all in order sweet & lovely. Men are sick with Love.[4]

What that last phrase testifies to, with its sudden change of idiom, as dramatic as Rilke's 'Du musst dein Leben ändern' in 'Archäischer Torso Apollos', is Blake's profound sense of life and the possibility of still more life. It is this conviction, this certainty of feeling, which sustains his most daring transitions from one moment to the next. At this moment in the poem, the phrase has the kind of life-sustaining force which is represented in Eliot's poetry by the poem 'Marina', the long-restrained but not denied feeling for

---

[1] *Ibid.*, p. 305. [2] *Ibid.*, p. 412. [3] *Ibid.*, p. 152. [4] *Ibid.*, pp. 520–1.

revelation, the transfiguration of experience. I associate it with another moment in Blake's *Milton*, when he says:

> Time is the mercy of Eternity; without Time's swiftness,
> Which is the swiftest of all things, all were eternal torment.[1]

And I associate both with the continuity of energy, desire, and action in Blake, a poet for whom these are congenial terms. There is in the Promethean imagination a temptation to drive the will beyond the human scale of action, a temptation which Allen Tate has called 'angelic', meaning that such an imagination places itself pretentiously above humanity.[2] Blake is subject to this temptation. He finds it hateful to accept that the imagination, which can do so much, cannot do everything. But often, too, he is protected from this excess by his feeling for the possible relations of human life, his sense of a moral form still possible to man: protected, too, by his transferring to process the motives which other poets fasten upon product and conclusion. Schiller says, in one of his letters on the aesthetic education of man, that 'in the eyes of a Reason which knows no limits, the Direction is at once the Destination, and the Way is completed from the moment it is trodden'.[3]

But these rival motives are simultaneously active in Blake, one does not happily stand aside in favour of the other. Blake was never willing to settle upon a form of unity, especially if it were offered under official auspices, until it had survived the challenge of multiplicity. If we say of the Prometheus myth that it may be interpreted with a choice of emphasis, we mean that we may emphasize the end, the gift of fire, or alternatively we may emphasize the act of theft; in the first we mark man's intellectual and spiritual possibilities, the paradigm of his development as a moral being, and in the second rather his recalcitrance, his self-determination, his naughtiness, and pride. Blake makes the second emphasis in the poem *America* where Orc speaks of 'the fiery joy, that

[1] *Ibid.*, p. 510.
[2] Allen Tate, *Essays of Four Decades*. London. Oxford University Press, 1970, p. 403.
[3] Schiller, *On the Aesthetic Education of Man*, edited and translated by Elizabeth M. Wilkinson and L. A. Willoughby. Oxford. Clarendon Press, 1967, p. 59.

Urizen perverted to ten commands'.[1] Reason's 'stony law' is set aside by the voice which says: 'For every thing that lives is holy, life delights in life'. The Romantic Promethean associates himself with a new beginning; as in *Prometheus Unbound* he takes the risk of contrariety, of revolution as a moral act. He proposes a vision of a new earth and a new man, of the God who speaks, as Blake says in the Introduction to *Jerusalem*, 'in thunder and in fire'. When we think of Blake as a prophetic poet, we think of him in such associations: the inspiration from these sources goes directly into the words, without the mediation of Nature or its silent forms. So far as prophecy has an object, it is, as Blake says in *Jerusalem*:

> To open the Eternal Worlds, to open the immortal Eyes
> Of Man inwards into the Worlds of Thought, into Eternity
> Ever expanding in the Bosom of God, the Human Imagination.[2]

So when Blake speaks, in the same poem, of keeping the Divine Vision in time of trouble, the trouble is the philosophy of five senses, empiricism, naturalism, the machine age, Urizen's stony sleep, imposed Law, the swoon into which Locke sank, according to one of Yeats's poems. The Divine Vision is kept by imagination, language, prophecy, creative freedom, and a sense of life as something lived not for mere self but for others: 'Man liveth not by Self alone, but in his brother's face'.[3] These values taken together I think of as the moral equivalent of metaphor, an answer to Hobbes, an assertion that we are not tied to the same dull round of self. The prophetic books are best understood as metaphors of imagination, its possibility set against the obstacles of self and a sullen world: its human enemies are those who conspire to keep the world in that sullen state. But the conflicts given in those books are not in the first instance conflicts of individual and society, they are struggles between rival motives in the same person. Blake's wars are civil wars in the first instance, even if thereafter they find their counterparts in the public world. I see no reason to assume that he is deploying motives already classified: while his heroes and villains are named, there are temptations to which he is still exposed, and much of the effort of the poems is to distinguish rival

---

[1] Blake, *Complete Writings*, p. 198.   [2] *Ibid.*, p. 623.   [3] *Ibid.*, p. 374.

forces which the poet feels within himself. It is natural for him to assume that such an effort has representative value.

I am arguing that there is in Blake's imagination a restless demon, extraordinarily sensitive to divisions and rivalries. When we respond to the passages in which the poet lays aside his trouble, it is because we know how powerfully, to achieve them, he had to curb his own spirit. But while his poetry enacts a civil war, it declares at the same time his confidence that he is a poet and that his chosen role cannot finally be set aside. This is what we have in mind when we are tempted to think that he is more important than anything he wrote; that, as Borges said with less justice of Valéry and Whitman, the work of such poets is less valuable as poetry than as the mark of an exemplary poet who was himself created by it. To Blake, writing is a revolutionary act, it requires a dynamic syntax, a syntax of process and fulfilment, more Hebraic than Greek, and its characteristic rhythms are those of desire and action. If it is easy to think of these poems as forms of violence, the reason is that their energy is organized as a sequence of acts. Every sentence is an act, an exercise of moral conviction. There is little evidence of hesitation or misgiving, whatever the degree of restlessness, because Blake ascribes to genius its proper certitude. 'What is now proved was once only imagin'd', he says, and a poet imagined it. There is a celebrated passage in Schiller about the daring of genius to rely upon itself, relaxing the censorship of reason at the threshold of consciousness. 'In the creative mind,' he says, 'the understanding has withdrawn its sentinels from the gates, the ideas rush in *pêle-mêle*, and only then does it scrutinize and review the whole company of them.'[1] A captious reader might say that a genius ought to keep his guards on duty, for the sake of good sense, but if we are to receive a work of Promethean genius, we must take its excess as part of its character, we cannot have the fiery joy by rule or measure. At this point we are thinking of Blake as a genius who speaks with exemplary force to our time. Some years ago Lionel Trilling argued that the modern con-

---

[1] Schiller, Letter to Körner, December 1, 1788, quoted in *On the Aesthetic Education of Man, supra*, p. 292.

sciousness requires its artists to exert an intransigent imagination, even to the extent that while we are under its influence the ordinary world will have no power over us but will seem 'the creation of some inferior imagination, that of mere convention and habit'.[1] Trilling spoke of Kafka as a typical artist according to this requirement, and of Hawthorne and James as imaginations not sufficiently ruthless in their relations to the ordinary world. At the same time he quoted Santayana as saying: 'Don't you understand by now that the real object of piety is matter – or Nature, if you prefer? It is the idea of Might – the ineluctable Yahveh of the Hebrew, when this primitive notion has been freed of its local and superstitious accretions.' And then Trilling supposed himself to hear the 'great offended voice' of Blake insisting upon the power of the artist's imagination 'to deny the reality of the primordial Might, or to challenge and overcome it, or to interpose between it and us a dream, which, perhaps in the degree that it terrifies, commands our assent and holds out the promise of freedom'. It is easy to think this impression of Blake just, except for one consideration, that his rhetoric would be mere bombast if it were not directed against a god of primordial Might, and against comparably terrible motives within himself. Blake makes of the imagination a power equal and opposite to that of the Hebraic God, as if that God were a rival form of imagination: one power is certified by another. He resents the natural world when it appears sullen or sufficient to itself or going its own way, independent of the imagination, and he denounces those weak men who yield themselves to the world. He does not require us to believe that the human imagination made the world, but that Nature's radiance to spiritual eyes depends upon the perceiver. Blake proposes a quarrel about value, not about chemistry or substance. I have not found any evidence that he interposes a dream between us and the God of Thunder: what he interposes is a continuous act of the imagination, not to terrify but to demonstrate what is possible. If the natural world is God's text, Blake does not offer to edit it or write notes along its margin; he insists

---

[1] Lionel Trilling, *Beyond Culture*. London. Secker and Warburg, 1966, p. 205.

upon writing a poem under his own authority and name, commensurate with the first text in majesty and force. The first text presents itself immediately in the form of appearances, the second in the form of relations: that is, Blake's imagination, since it distinguishes itself so strictly from the sensory power, is not primarily concerned with the appearances of things, but with their possible or ideal relations, given the primary authority of the imagination. These relations are defined in the prophetic poems, where names and characters are ascribed to the several motives engaged. Blake is not, then, a descriptive poet, except incidentally when he finds the natural phenomena moving according to patterns incipiently aesthetic. He is a prescriptive poet, concerned with justice and injustice, love and self, plenitude and poverty.

I have quoted Schiller and will do so again. His celebrated distinction between naive and sentimental poets is hardly acceptable in those terms, but his account of the naive poet is suggestive in its bearing upon Romantic literature in general. He says for instance that the naive genius has to do everything through his nature, he can do little or nothing through his freedom. The naive genius can accomplish his art only when Nature works in him from inner necessity. I think of Wordsworth as a poet who does his work through his nature, with only as much recourse to his freedom as is consistent with the prior recognition of his nature. He chooses to remain within his nature, and this choice is the only freedom he takes: thereafter, he explores what he has recognized as his proper world, and is happy or miserable with the evidence of that relation. He is content when his sense of his own nature coincides with his sense of the nature of things, when both laws are identical; he is miserable when he senses a division of natures, and his own appears sullen, out of tune. Blake, on the other hand, insists upon doing everything through his freedom, and he appeals to his nature no more than he appeals to Reason, since both powers are understood as given and limited. The distinction between nature and freedom is particularly useful if we think of it along with the distinction which Yeats proposed betwen character and personality. Character is what we are given, it comes to us like a birthmark; personality is what our imagination makes of character,

when it exerts its freedom. The doctrine of the mask in Wilde
and Yeats is merely a plan of acting through one's freedom rather
than through one's nature. Yeats's *A Vision* is an attempt to construe the evidence of human history by setting freedom against
nature and fate: we think the book fanciful or deterministic
according as we respond more forcefully to one factor rather than
the other. But Wordsworth's concern is to trace the affinities
between his nature, human nature in general, and the nature of the
universe, adding such conclusions about the nature of God as the
evidence appears to warrant. In the first Book of *The Prelude* he
speaks of 'those first-born affinities that fit / Our new existence to
existing things', and his theme is their blended might. This does
not mean that his poems are merely essays in self-satisfaction: no
poet is more sensitive than Wordsworth to the hazards of feeling,
the risks a person takes in being a person, which are only different
in degree from the risks a poet takes in being a poet:

> We Poets in our youth begin in gladness;
> But thereof comes in the end despondency and madness.

I am sure that readers of that poem, 'Resolution and Independence',
do not chiefly recall it for the comparatively serene ending which
it reaches: they are more likely to think of the starkness of the
scene, its bareness and exposure. At the same time the purpose of
the incident which the poem recites is to stabilize the up-and-down
of joy and despondency, the insecurity and caprice of feeling as
given in the early stanzas. The poem has the effect, at last, of
reconciling the poet to his circumstances, which include the threat
of madness as much as the satisfactions of landscape; the presence
of the leech-gatherer has this in view. Wordsworth's aim is to
prove to himself that moral experience is continuous with sensory
experience; this is not the same thing as saying that moral experience may be reduced to sensory experience. At the end, the leech-
gatherer comes to fill the entire space of the poem, the interior
landscape, and we feel that he has taken the strain of all the
experiences, however diverse, touched upon in the poem. In turn,
Wordsworth is now assured, as Blake would have scorned to

assure himself, that some part of the human burden may be sustained by others, that a man who acts through his nature can call upon the general continuity of nature for help and consolation.

The contrast with Blake arises from this difference. The Promethean poet feels that the fate of the world depends upon him alone, he must not seek help or sign treaties. In Romantic literature generally Prometheus becomes 'the poet', guardian of intellectual Beauty, the mind speaking in its own cause against an increasingly materialistic world. The 'figure of the youth as virile poet' becomes the heroic figure, determined to free the world from its slavery. In the Preface to *Prometheus Unbound* Shelley says of the reconciliation supposed to obtain between Zeus and Prometheus at the end of Aeschylus's trilogy that he was averse to 'a catastrophe so feeble as that of reconciling the Champion with the Oppressor of mankind'. Comparing Prometheus with Milton's Satan, Shelley goes on to say that Prometheus was a more poetical character than Satan because 'exempt from the taints of ambition, envy, revenge, and a desire for personal aggrandisement which, in the Hero of *Paradise Lost*, interfere with the interest'. Shelley thought Milton's Satan too bourgeois, too concerned with getting on in the world, and therefore not good enough to be a poetic ideal. Prometheus, he says, is 'the type of the highest perfection of moral and intellectual nature, impelled by the purest and the truest motives to the best and noblest ends'.[1] What Shelley's drama proposes is nothing less than a revision of man's moral history, a new beginning. The play does not speak of knowledge, reason, or vision: its most original interpretation of the myth renounces that idiom and replaces it by the idiom of love, the human love which, Shelley says, 'makes all it gazes on Paradise'. The fire is the fire of love, not the fire of knowledge. Zeus is the old tyrant, and he must be defeated, but not by cunning or zeal. The true drama is that which brings together Prometheus and his emanation, Asia. The world is to become 'One brotherhood', the principle of Love will release man from subjection to chance and mutability. The prophecy of love which the Spirit of Earth speaks in the fourth

---

[1] Shelley, *Selected Poetry*, pp. 61–2.

Act is a hymn to intellectual beauty, to a new world formed as if
it were a poem:

> Language is a perpetual Orphic song,
> Which rules with Daedal harmony a throng
> Of thoughts and forms, which else senseless and shapeless were.[1]

So the play is less a play than a ballet of aspiration, in which
motives are translated according to a formula given in the *Defence
of Poetry*, where Shelley says that poetry 'compels us to feel that
which we perceive, and to imagine that which we know'. It is as
if he were content to trust the empiricists with what we perceive,
and the rationalists with what we know, but then to translate
these possessions into the higher, Platonic language of poetry. The
continuity with Blake is clear, though it does not encourage us to
make a closer comparison of their poetries. The main difference
is that Shelley's poetry, sooner than Blake's, would disengage the
objects of attention from their presence in the given world.
Shelley's poetry is more impatient than Blake's to leave the world
and to replace it by a figment compounded of discontent and
aspiration. Blake's poetry, though it is often thought wilful, is
readier than Shelley's to acknowledge the weight of fact and
history. The quarrel between Orc and Urizen, for instance, in the
seventh Night of *Vala* could not have been written without Blake's
sense of Reason's daily *realpolitik*. When Orc says:

> King of furious hail storms,
> Art thou the cold attractive power that holds me in this chain?
> I well remember how I stole thy light & it became fire
> Consuming . . .

the effect of his wrath depends upon its issuing from the Machiavel-
lian expertise of Urizen, the skill and the 'soft mild arts' by which
he compels 'the poor to live upon a Crust of bread'. Blake and
Shelley are poets of revolution, but Blake does not assume, as
Shelley often does, that to make a revolution it is sufficient to
aspire. The Promethean motive is active in both poets, but in
Blake it is consistent with conflict, in Shelley it is an incitement to
enthusiasm. Shelley is a gesture, Blake is an act.

---

[1] *Ibid.*, p. 123.

The Peremptory Imagination

It will hardly be denied that the Promethean motive is active in the Romantic imagination generally: it may even be present in Wordsworth's imagination, though I have not found it there. Where it is present in other poets, it is found in close relation to certain motives which are hard to distinguish, except in extreme cases: individualism, idealism, Satanism, symbolism, the poet's hostility to bourgeois society. The myth of Prometheus, like the Satan of *Paradise Lost*, is almost too readily available to poets who place supreme value upon the Romantic figure of the hero: too readily available, because Prometheus does not criticize himself, does not detect himself. The first quality of this rebel is that he thinks his rebellion self-evidently justified; he sins, but condemns the justice which punishes him. He does not confess himself even partly at fault. This means that he reduces all his motives to one, which then becomes his identity; there is no remainder, because he has no misgivings. He is the force concentrated in his name. Indeed, one of the marks of Blake's genius is that while its motives often took a Promethean form, they were not exhausted by that form. Blake's energy was not content to be expressed, it demanded to be provoked, it took up arms against itself.

This has been denied, notably by Eliot in a famous essay. Eliot began by acknowledging that 'Blake's poetry has the unpleasantness of great poetry',[1] and by relating that unpleasantness to Blake's honesty. But as he proceeded, though the essay is brief, he took back with one hand what he had given with the other. The lyrics are approved, they are short and impassioned, they do not go wrong. But in the long prophetic poems, according to Eliot's argument, Blake runs to ideas when he should have been minding his proper business, the poetry, its form, its rhythm. 'About Blake's supernatural territories, as about the supposed ideas that dwell there', Eliot says, 'we cannot help commenting on a certain meanness of culture'. It is a shocking phrase, and the sting of it cannot be removed by any amount of sweetness before or after. Kathleen Raine tried to refute Eliot by saying that a culture 'embracing Plato and Plotinus, the Bible and the *Hermetica*, English science

---

[1] T. S. Eliot, *Selected Essays*. London. Faber and Faber, 1951, pp. 321–2.

and philosophy, the tradition of Alchemy, Gibbon and Herodotus, besides the body of English poetry – not to mention his equally wide knowledge of painting – can scarcely be called mean'.[1] But that is not what Eliot meant at all: he was not reflecting upon the range of Blake's reading or even upon his powers of assimilation, he was concerned with Blake's individual talent, his genius, and the charge that, as Eliot thought, his genius was not disciplined or modified by what he read. 'What his genius required, and what it sadly lacked,' Eliot maintained, 'was a framework of accepted and traditional ideas which would have prevented him from indulging in a philosophy of his own, and concentrated his attention upon the problems of the poet.' Eliot would have conceded that Blake's reading in the literature of alchemy, philosophy, and history gave him metaphors for his poetry, but he argued that it did not give Blake what he needed, a principle of intellectual and moral discipline issuing from sources acknowledged as greater than his genius. That is why Eliot thought Blake merely a poet of genius, not a classic. Eliot registers only one complaint against Blake, but it is so large that it covers nearly everything: that Blake did not subject himself to the force of a moral tradition, to what Eliot a few years later called 'orthodoxy'. In *After Strange Gods*, where he does not reflect upon Blake at all, Eliot made another attempt to enforce the values of tradition as a restraint upon the wilfulness of individual talent. He associated tradition with orthodoxy while disclaiming a theological intention, and he distinguished the terms to the extent of saying that many elements of tradition are bound to be unconscious, while 'the maintenance of orthodoxy is a matter which calls for the exercise of all our conscious intelligence'.[2] In the years between 'Tradition and the Individual Talent' and *After Strange Gods* Eliot moved close to the position of identifying virtue with consciousness: this is why, of two congenial terms, he preferred 'orthodoxy' to 'tradition'. Orthodoxy, he said, 'represents a consensus between the living and the dead',

---

[1] Kathleen Raine, 'Blake's Debt to Antiquity', *Sewanee Review*, Vol. LXXI, No. 3, Summer 1963, pp. 449–450.

[2] T. S. Eliot, *After Strange Gods*. London. Faber and Faber, 1934, p. 28.

a consensus issuing in consciousness, self-discipline, and humility. It is in that sense that Eliot praised Joyce as 'the most ethically orthodox of the more eminent writers of my time', because Joyce acknowledged the pressure of orthodoxy upon his talent. The fact that he rejected religious belief and religious practice so far as his private life was concerned only makes his acknowledgement of orthodoxy, in the artistic sense, the more remarkable.

There is another passage in Eliot which throws some light, indirectly, upon his attitude to Blake: this is a consideration of Balzac and Dostoevsky as artists in whose imaginations the fantastic element is important. Eliot maintained that 'Dostoevsky's point of departure is always a human brain in a human environment, and the "aura" is simply the continuation of the quotidian experience of the brain into seldom explored extremities of torture'. That is, 'Dostoevsky begins with the real world . . . he only pursues reality farther in a certain direction'. But 'in Balzac the fantastic element is of another sort: it is not an extension of reality, it is an atmosphere thrown upon reality direct from the personality of the writer'. 'If we ask ourselves in relation to what real solid object the "atmosphere" of Balzac has meaning, the incantation is powerless.'[1] Eliot's complaint against Blake arises from the same source, that the art is self-indulgent, too much of Blake's 'atmosphere' is thrown upon reality direct from the writer's personality: not enough arises from the disciplined pursuit of reality.

It is difficult to mediate. Eliot's attitude to Blake is consistent with his suspicion of Prometheans in general: he distrusts revolutionary acts, he values all those conservative forces which restrain the flow of feeling and action. The real problem of Romantic literature is that poets felt compelled to assert the primacy of imagination against what they felt as the combined force of reason, memory, empiricism, science, and law. The poets felt that they were the sole guardians of a creative power, a mode of freedom abused by the merely hereditary forces of society. This had the effect, largely unfortunate, of setting the poetic character

---

[1] T.S.E., 'Beyle and Balzac', *The Atheneum*, May 30, 1919, p. 392.

against the public forms of order, tradition, and orthodoxy: these were felt as residual manifestations of brute nature, beyond cultural redemption. About the theory of the creative imagination there is nothing new to be said, except perhaps that it is a tautology, it supplies the answer in the manner in which it formulates the question: it is the poet's version of idealism, and in extreme cases the poet's version of solipsism. Fortunately, extreme cases are rare, and Blake is not one of them. We have only to read *Milton* or *Jerusalem* to see that he is not a wild man, perpetrator of arbitrary fictions or self-induced fantasies. He was not willing to subject himself to orthodoxy, in Eliot's sense, but there is indisputable evidence that he bound himself to the laws of the English language, the vernacular idiom, and the moral pressure implicit in grammar and syntax. I make no apology for including the word 'moral' in that category because I maintain that there are sanctions implicit in grammar and syntax which bear upon the poet as a code of manners bears upon a gentleman. It is always a difficult matter to say how much discipline an artist needs. Eliot felt that such writers as Blake, Hardy, Yeats, and Lawrence were too easy with themselves in that regard, and that as a result their characteristic work is wilful and egotistical. I think this says more about Eliot himself than about the several writers impugned: it describes his own art in terms of the conditions he imposed upon it, rather than their art in terms of indulgence. There is also Eliot's philosophic contempt for ideas and thoughts, which as a student of Bradley he regarded as merely decayed forms of feeling. What commonly passes for thought is merely a corrupt substitute for feeling: so Eliot distrusted any poet who appeared to set up shop as a thinker. This is a long story. I mention it only for its bearing upon the question of a writer's genius and the discipline it may or may not accept. The question is crucial in the case of a writer who acts through his freedom rather than through his nature. What we require, in the way of discipline, is that such a force lie as lightly as possible upon a writer's talent, but that it lie heavily enough to make the exercise of talent legal. The writer should not be aware of it, except when he is tempted to ignore it. I think of this discipline as operating like a code of manners, we refer to it only when we are tempted not to. John Crowe Ransom has remarked that 'the function of a code of manners is to make us capable of something better than the stupidity of an appetitive or economic life', and he has related the observance of forms to the observance of a code of manners by saying that 'the object of a proper society is to instruct its members how to transform instinctive experience into aesthetic experience'.[1] In other words; how to transform their nature into culture. I cannot see how Blake's poems can be denied the merit of that aim, or the merit of a code of manners adequate to the feelings engaged. As a poet, he had no more respect than Eliot had for the purely instinctive experience, since such a thing was merely nature, not culture. Eliot's sense of orthodoxy makes it a more specific bond, more legal in its operation than anything prescribed by Blake, apart from loyalty to the freedom of imagination. In 'Little Gidding' and elsewhere Eliot finds ancestral values at work in a poet's grammar, 'where every word is at home, / Taking its place to support the others', and most readers are likely to accept that version of discipline rather than a more particular orthodoxy. I assume that Eliot's strictures upon Blake include his impression that Blake does not sufficiently acknowledge the discipline of form and pattern, the spiritual exercise of 'stillness'. Blake's freedom he thought ostentatious: this is what his strictures come to, it is a question of the laws a poet needs to obey. In his later years Eliot preferred laws to be written and therefore authoritative, because he preferred, among the virtues, humility and obedience, the abatement of pride and will. It is my impression that Blake thought the best laws implicit in the continuity of a major language, like rituals in a major religion, certified by imaginative choice and freedom. The language a writer uses is mostly conventional and hereditary; one writer is normally distinguished from another by a flick of feeling, a characteristic nuance of style. The writer is granted such liberty because he has sufficiently observed the laws of the language, he has acknowledged the code and the values implicit in it. Blake's

---

[1] John Crowe Ransom, *The World's Body*. Baton Rouge. University of Louisiana Press, 1968, pp. 34, 42.

style is new in particular but old in general: more precisely, his style is a personal relation between new and old. His assertion of liberty is more extreme in theory than in practice, because in practice he respects while in theory he derides his inheritance, the consensus of a people expressed in their language. Eliot may have taken Blake's theory too seriously, and his practice not seriously enough; his way of not taking it seriously was to find it vitiated by ideas, and loose in its freedom. I think he was too suspicious on that occasion, too rigid in his insistence that forms must be orthodox. In practice, Blake acknowledges, as Eliot does, the relation between one's own idiolect and the dialect of the tribe. The last problem remains, that Blake's characteristic feeling was revolutionary or Promethean, and that Eliot's was not. Eliot was not a 'Wordsworthian' poet, he did not ground his poetry upon a treaty with natural phenomena. His quarrel with Blake turns upon a question of scruple, in other words upon a question of the relative values of feeling, will, and order. I see no way of making peace between them on that score.

Thieves of Fire

'Donc le poëte est vraiment
voleur de feu.'

                – Rimbaud to Paul Demeny,
                May 15, 1871.

IN 1855 Herman Melville wrote a story called 'The Bell-Tower',
a parable on the question of techniques and values. The
'mechanician' Bannadonna builds a stone tower and sets upon
it a great bell. He is to make a mechanical man to strike the bell
every hour, but in fact he creates an automaton called Haman, a
new and greater man while still man's servant. In the event, the
creature kills his creator. The narrator says that to Bannadonna
'common sense was theurgy; machinery, miracle; Prometheus,
the heroic name for machinist; man, the true God'.[1] The story is
a slight thing, hardly more than a footnote to the great American
question of energy and moral choice. But I want to turn it slightly
askew, so that it faces another nineteenth-century predicament, or
the same one presenting a different guise. Let us say that 'The Bell-
Tower' is merely Melville's version of *Frankenstein*, with at least
this justification, that both are concerned with Promethean energies,
motives dangerously cut loose or running wild in the world,
caprices indulged, energies monstrously in excess, beyond human
need or use. Mary Shelley is inspired by the Prometheus who
created mankind, infusing life into clay: her modern Prometheus
is a chemist, with alchemy still in his veins. Whatever difficulty
Victor Frankenstein encountered in creating his monster, Mary
Shelley found it easy enough to create both the monster and his
creator; she had only to start with the wilful imagination, the
alchemical dream of creating life, and then to add the modern
proliferation of energies, idle and therefore dangerous. The only
difficulty, we may suppose, was that of ending the story, disposing
of those energies. Mary Shelley could not face her own logic.
When the monster has killed Frankenstein, he is supreme, and

---

[1] Herman Melville, *Selected Tales and Poems*, ed. Richard Chase. New York.
Rinehart, 1955, p. 203.

there is no reason why he should not roam the world, destroying the race which condemned him to solitude. Mary Shelley makes him repent, as if energy could weep, and he goes off to consume himself in fire: the 'vital spark' chooses to extinguish itself, for the good of mankind. The story ends with that desperately pious hope.

If we bring 'The Bell-Tower' and *Frankenstein* together, we are encouraged to see that both stories are concerned with the will run wild, gorging itself on possibility, regardless of the end. Whatever is possible is for that reason necessary, especially to chemists. What the liberated will creates is, in both stories, a separate form of energy, only ostensibly man's slave and in the end not his slave at all but his tyrant. But suppose the will were to create not a monster separate from itself but a monstrous form of itself, so that the two personalities live violently together under a single name and within the same body. Then there are several possibilities: the two personalities may engage in that civil war to the end, with victory for either party, as in the case of Dostoevsky's 'doubles', those characters who live by the violence of contradiction. Do we not feel, when we read Dostoevsky's novels of crime and mania, that the chief characters are beside themselves, the first person singular is at the same time a second person equally singular, that one is really two, each palpable as the other's shadow? There is another possibility; that the second person may already have engorged the first, when the story begins, so that the first remains only as a memory or an improbable possibility, which might still be recovered, like a suppressed conscience. Do we not feel, reading *Moby-Dick*, that Melville's imagination is inspired by his sense of a ghostly presence surrounding the visible body of man, a second man created by the first in pride and rage until the second engulfs the first and nothing of the first remains but its testimony in other men? Thus Ahab is distinguished from other men who have no shadows, no ghosts, being first persons without ambiguity; especially Ishmael and Starbuck. In Ahab, the first person is nearly destroyed, like his body, and the second is nearly all there is, except for its intermittent sense of what it has destroyed, making way for itself.

Melville puts this notion into our minds in *Moby-Dick* when

Thieves of Fire

Ahab speaks of the blacksmith as Prometheus:

> I do deem it now a most meaning thing, that that old Greek, Prometheus, who made men, they say, should have been a blacksmith, and animated them with fire; for what's made in fire must properly belong to fire: and so hell's probable.[1]

And then Ahab plays the conceit of ordering his Prometheus to make a new man, a monster with 'no heart at all, brass forehead, and about a quarter of an acre of fine brains'. The conceit is not developed, for in a sense it has already been given in other terms. I find it active in *Moby-Dick* wherever the book speaks of division, or represents the essential doubleness or duplicity of man. Sometimes it is given as the division of soul and body, shadow and substance, as when Ishmael says, 'Methinks that what they call my shadow here on earth is my true substance . . . Methinks my body is but the lees of my better being'.[2] This is a harmless fiction, its Platonism entirely compatible with the requirements of common sense: it can be indulged along with that unconscious reverie which Melville describes later in the book as 'the blending cadence of waves with thoughts', the happy mood in which the dreamer 'takes the mystic ocean at his feet for the visible image of that deep, blue, bottomless soul, pervading mankind and nature'.[3] It testifies not to danger in itself but to the possibility of another danger, sinister where the first is nearly innocent: the other danger is mooted, though still merely mooted, when Melville, describing an early encounter between Ahab and the white whale, says that as a result 'his torn body and gashed soul bled into one another; and so interfusing, made him mad'.[4] Meanwhile, and especially in the early chapters, Melville lets Ishmael hold these divisions in easy abeyance, there is no hurry, they will assert themselves in good time. It is enough if the sound of division is heard from time to time, however amiably; as when Ishmael says, 'Because no man can ever feel his own identity aright except his eyes be closed; as if darkness were indeed the proper element of our essences, though

---

[1] Melville, *Moby-Dick or, The Whale*, eds. Luther S. Mansfield and Howard P. Vincent. New York. Hendricks House, 1962, pp. 466–7.

[2] *Ibid.*, p. 36.   [3] *Ibid.*, pp. 156–7.   [4] *Ibid.*, p. 182.

light be more congenial to our clayey part'.[1] Existence and essence, darkness and light, our soul and our clayey part: it is enough, at this stage, to have such terms moving about, genially enough, for the violence they will incite later on. The same applies to the question of land and sea. Mostly in Melville, as in Conrad, land is the place of happy lies, day-dreams; sea is the place of truth, freedom, moral choice. In a famous chapter Melville speaks of 'that mortally intolerable truth; that all deep, earnest thinking is but the intrepid effort of the soul to keep the open independence of her sea; while the wildest winds of heaven and earth conspire to cast her on the treacherous, slavish shore'. 'But as in landlessness alone resides the highest truth, shoreless, indefinite as God – so, better is it to perish in that howling infinite, than be ingloriously dashed upon the lee, even if that were safety! For worm-like, then, oh! who would craven crawl to land!'[2] In a later chapter Melville develops the notion that just as 'this appalling ocean surrounds the verdant land, so in the soul of man there lies one insular Tahiti, full of peace and joy, but encompassed by all the horrors of the half known life'.[3] This version of pastoral is allowed to stand with others, only to be overwhelmed at last. Finally, or finally for our purpose, there are the divisions and analogies between man and Nature: 'not the smallest atom stirs or lives on matter, but has its cunning duplicate in mind'.[4]

I am suggesting that in the first half of the book Melville is content to deploy his cunning duplicates; body and soul, land and sea, shadow and substance, matter and mind. They are meant to be significant, and they are, but not portentous or exorbitant at this stage. Melville does not want to take the harm out of them, but he makes sure not to put too much harm into them, until the right time comes when they swell with all the harm in the world. The duplicates are separate and are kept apart until their separateness is overwhelmed in a sinister unity, compounded of transgression and will. That is why they are given to the reader in the categories provided for him by literary convention: he is to receive them in conventional terms until such terms are con-

---

[1] *Ibid.*, p. 53.   [2] *Ibid.*, p. 105.   [3] *Ibid.*, p. 274.   [4] *Ibid.*, p. 310.

founded and he is left with nothing but his affronted sensibility. More important, the same duplicates are given to Ahab, so that he can strike through them. Melville's strategy is to present Ahab, at the beginning, in simple melodramatic terms, the star-crazed captain, two parts legend to one of proof: and then to concentrate his fictive life until there is nothing there but his purpose. That purpose, by its intensity, becomes a second person, at this stage a criminal successor to the first. The crucial passage comes in Chapter XLIV:

> But as the mind does not exist unless leagued with the soul, there it must have been that, in Ahab's case, yielding up all his thoughts and fancies to his own supreme purpose; that purpose, by its own sheer inveteracy of will, forced itself against gods and devils into a kind of self-assumed, independent being of its own. Nay, could grimly live and burn, while the common vitality to which it was conjoined, fled horror-stricken from the unbidden and un-fathered birth . . . God help thee, old man, thy thoughts have created a creature in thee; a vulture feeds upon that heart for ever; that vulture the very creature he creates.[1]

Ahab is Promethean because he consumes his history in his purpose, he is determined to destroy that history for the sake of his purpose. He forces experience to concentrate itself or to deny itself for the sake of his single motive: his mind never expands to meet experience, and we feel that it has transfixed itself in the creation of its second self. All that can happen now is that the second self will obliterate the first, or nearly so. Meanwhile Ahab is set off against Ishmael, for Ishmael represents the genial weaving of free-dom and necessity, and there is a chapter called 'The Mat-Maker' to prove it. Ishmael is the still point of the turning world, the calm centre: 'amid the tornadoed Atlantic of my being, do I myself still for ever centrally disport in mute calm; and while ponderous planets of unwaning woe revolve round me, deep down and deep inland there I still bathe me in eternal mildness of joy'.[2] This is not, indeed, the whole truth of Ishmael, for he represents the common sense driven wild, for a time, turning upon itself in frenzy before it reverts to its nature in the end. He feels Ahab's madness, because it

[1] *Ibid.*, p. 200. [2] *Ibid.*, p. 387.

touches him in fits and starts: but his statutory role brings him back on course. He is a sane man, susceptible to nightmare. Ahab is set off, too, against Starbuck, a staid, sensible man, domestic in his inclinations, with 'the soft feeling of the human in me', a reasonable man mediating between land and sea. Ahab is distinguished from Queequeg, who is associated with chance, 'chance, free will, and necessity – no wise incompatible', as Ishmael says of him. The other distinctions are obvious, it is not necessary to recite them, they go all the way from Starbuck to Fedallah, Ahab's harpooner, his malign shadow, and whatever Fedallah stands for it must be as close to Ahab as his will. If there is anything closer to Ahab than that, it is his sense of what he shares with Pip, reason in madness to begin with until reason is drowned in madness, Pip's idiot laughter, Ahab's roar of pride.

These are relations, important only as light is important to shadow: except for Fedallah and Pip, they are not important to Ahab. Or, more precisely, in relation to Ahab these people and these relations stand for what is of no account, except provisionally. At the beginning, they have the worth of instruments, but near the end they have lost even that, they stand for everything in the world that is now of no account. They are meant to drop away, to recede, while we race along beside Ahab and take his vision as our own. In that sense they stand for us, our common vitality, and as the book progressively makes them obsolete, so it gives us a corresponding fate: a crucial experience in reading the book is to find our common values rendered obsolete as we are forced more and more to sacrifice our sense of life to Ahab's. Ishmael, Starbuck and Queequeg are what Ahab strikes through, when he strikes at the gods, though he says he strikes only through the white whale. Sometimes Ahab complains that necessity rules in the form of fate, and free will is a delusion: sometimes he turns that complaint around, making it now a justification for his deed, as if to say it is written and must be fulfilled. But when he smashes the quadrant, he rejects everything that sends a man's eyes above the horizon. The only relation he accepts is his relation to his element, the spirit of fire. 'Oh, thou clear spirit, of thy fire thou madest me, and like a true child of fire, I breathe it back to thee.'

To the lightning he cries: 'defyingly I worship thee!'[1] Fire is the unitary element, it destroys difference, it sponsors the release of essence from existence, it is the element most congenial to blasphemy and daring. Thus Bachelard gave the name 'Promethean' to all those tendencies which drive us to know more than our fathers. And thus, too, Rimbaud said that the poet is a thief of fire. What is implicit in both is a suggestion of consciousness going beyond the mark in disobedience and defiance; and, in Rimbaud, the poet as sponsor of those determinations. In that case, the role of the poet as seer (*voyant*) is handed over as if to a second self. When Rimbaud spoke of making himself a seer through 'all forms of love, suffering, and madness', what did he mean except that the poet must create, as if beside himself, a second person, artificial, the result of that celebrated 'rational derangement of all the senses' (par un long, immense et raisonné *dérèglement* de *tous les sens*) which he proclaimed? Love, suffering, and madness in that case differ from their common forms only because they are willed, the results of risk and daring, rather than painful accidents. It is the will that makes the second person distinct from the first: the first bears experience, the second seeks it, challenges it to do its worst.

But we have to press much harder upon our theme. I have said that in *Moby-Dick* the second self has almost overwhelmed the first, from the beginning. I have also suggested that most of the characters, apart from Ahab, Fedallah, and Pip, are there to fill a void: or, more accurately, to give the reader the impression, at least provisionally, that there is substance everywhere and no void. But by bringing these two notions together, we see that they must be pressed further. Not only the minor characters, but everything else as well, is given as provisional. What is given is what in the end does not matter, or matters only ostensibly. The whale is what matters, because it is what cannot be denied. Ahab's passion matters, and his second self as the bearer and hero of that passion, but nothing else matters. For Ishmael, the business of whaling, with its attendant satisfaction, is enough: he gives himself to it as

---

[1] *Ibid.*, pp. 500–1.

to a sufficient reality, and when his feeling, conjured by Ahab's passion, flies beyond the business in hand, it affronts itself. But to Ahab, and increasingly to the reader, the business of whaling stands for all those values which are merely provisional or relative or circumstantial: it is that which drops away when true reality appears, as the whale appears. The whaling stands for everything in the world which engages one's interest, subject to the qualification that it leaves one's deepest interest famished. It is what one attends to, and rightly, but intermediately, biding one's time, until the time of truth comes. It is what is immediately there, and therefore inescapable; or at least it cannot be escaped by first persons. Melville takes the whaling seriously, and we are meant to follow him in doing so, but this is his justification for not finding in it the ground of truth. The whaling stands for everything that satisfies the first person by engaging his interest, but for that very reason it stands for everything which at last is seen to drop away. Reverting to an earlier idiom, we say that it is as if the body were to mean everything that matters at first and for a while, but not thereafter and at last; the body, meaning also the world of ordinary relations, common vitality, time and place. Only the soul remains, according to that conceit. We are speaking here of man's rage to transcend his nature: he can only do it by eliminating his history, presenting it as irrelevant, part of a stranger's life. If he gives reasons, therefore, the reasons are false. History, to such a man, is what is no longer valid, it is what attaches itself like rust to the first person, and like that person it must be transcended.

The whaling is important, therefore, but only as an interest which appears to fill a void, the appearance being deceptive. The white whale itself, according to many readers, symbolizes Evil, but I read it as symbolizing limits, the wall, the hard circumference of things, as well as everything contained in Robert Lowell's 'IS, the whited monster' in 'The Quaker Graveyard in Nantucket'. It is life itself, and beyond it there is nothing, the void. Ahab refuses limits and is driven mad by that refusal. When we think of his motive as vengeance, we mean it in the sense that the limited, finite world is felt as a transgression, an offence against the essential

Ahab, his soul. 'Aye, breach your last to the sun, Moby-Dick!' Ahab cries when the whale throws itself aloft like a salmon in the glittering air, and we feel that Ahab is challenging a second enemy, nature, the earth as 'an old chaos of the sun'. Ahab seeks vengeance against Moby-Dick not for a local offence but for the first of all offences; that life is finite, that man is not God, that we are granted a first person and create a second at our peril. Let us say that Reason is the name given to the mind insofar as it acknowledges limits and observes a corresponding decorum; and Vision is the name given to the mind insofar as it refuses limits and defines its decorum in that refusal. Therefore the human action which is mimed in *Moby-Dick* is the rage for essence, the rage which drives a man to dispossess himself of every finite good because he will settle for nothing less than the infinite, whether good or bad. And Melville's problem as an artist is to find a language for all this, a language close to things, so long as things are understood as the true signs of reality; but another language, or the same one *in extremis*, which disengages itself from attendance upon things when mere things drop away: at that point, the language must either sustain itself above the void or reach out for styles and conventions which have already served comparably extravagant purposes; the Bible, Shakespeare, *Paradise Lost*, Carlyle, the Browne of *Urn-Burial* and the *Religio Medici*. Nearly any language will do, so long as it gives an impression of need and risk and, sometimes, rapture. And while Melville pretends to hand over everything to his narrator, Ishmael, it is only pretence, entertained for what it is worth: it is worth nothing when the credences of common vitality and ordinary relations drop away and first persons are overwhelmed by their seconds: in those pages, Melville goes beyond Ishmael into omniscience, or dismisses Ishmael for the moment; either explanation is true. Ishmael, the guardian of the ordinary world, cannot conspire with passions he does not share or understand, they have pressed him as far as he can go, so he must be replaced by the greater consciousness represented by an epic language. The point is that Melville never knows on his own account precisely how much he can put into his words and therefore how much he has to leave out. He knows that what he leaves

out or consigns to the void is crucial because it is everything that
rejects the light of consciousness, it is the old mole in the cellar of
the unconscious and finally it is the whole cellar. The only value
of the words is to show where the light ends and the void begins.
Beyond that point, you can only consign to God or the Devil
whatever has not got into the words; with Melville in *Moby-Dick*
the true meaning is in the void, that Pandora's Box which we call
the unconscious when we think of any individual's portion of it
but which has no name when we think of it at large. We might as
well call it the *anima mundi* or the collective unconscious, it is
where words fail. One of the astonishing feats of *Moby-Dick* is to
give the reader a sense of truth as living a secret life 'where there is
nothing'; a sense of feeling as teased and confounded by anything
that can be produced to represent it. It is a question, as nearly every
question in literature is, of consciousness and experience, and the
gap between them. One of the characteristics of the Promethean
hero is that he refuses to allow such a gap, he insists that his consciousness will go all the way, up and down, as the essential spirit
of his experience. We say of modern literature that in it consciousness has engrossed experience: one result is that the modern
Promethean hero has given up his traditional role; he is no longer
to be seen in public, exercising his will upon experience to the
degree of destroying it. The Promethean motive has moved inside
consciousness itself, its pride now takes a reflexive form. It is not
that the hero abstains from the old defiance, but rather that he
watches himself abstaining, to the degree of insolence. The
Promethean motive is now the pride of self-consciousness, and the
play is performed in private, within the mind. The play is just as
theatrical as it ever was, just as pretentious, if we choose to dis-
approve of it, and certainly just as liable to the vanity of self. René
Girard has said of Valéry's M. Teste that he is merely a dandy in
the realm of intelligence, 'he abstains from desire in order that we
should desire his mind'.[1] The dandy is the hero of his private play,

---

[1] René Girard, *Deceit, Desire and the Novel*, tr. Yvonne Freccero. Baltimore. Johns
Hopkins Press, 1965, p. 279.

a play of mind in excess, of feeling in aberration. He is the Promethean in straits, true to himself in one respect at least, that he drives his consciousness all the way, whatever its fortune in the public world.

I have been speaking of the obsolescence, in *Moby-Dick*, of those ostensible tokens of reality which are given in the whaling, the marine procedures, the crew, and so on. I want to suggest now that this pattern is common and perhaps inevitable in Promethean fictions, even in fictions in which the Promethean motive is eventually disowned. Prometheus defied Zeus, and committed himself to his own will. In nineteenth-century fiction, where the question of God is often reduced to the question of social and personal relations, the Promethean hero is defined by his rejecting such amenities, he finds them contemptible. They would satisfy him in his first person, perhaps, but not in his second, his self-created demon. That the demon can be satisfied by nothing in the given world is only to be expected; it can only be satisfied by its invented forms, the expense of its own energy. I choose *Crime and Punishment* for an example. Many chapters of that novel offer to account for Raskolnikov's killing the old woman Alyona Ivanovna by showing various reasons: his illness, pride, poverty, the stench of his life, the obnoxiousness of the old woman, the force of chance which told him that she would be alone in her room at seven o'clock on a particular evening, his sense of fateful coincidence, and so on. But these reasons are given only to be refuted, they are not cancelled but rendered obsolete. They would have been valid reasons in another novel, given another motive. In this novel, they are given only in default of other tangible reasons, and so that they may drop away to reveal the true reason, however intangible, the nature of Raskolnikov's will, which he calls his Napoleonism. The pattern is given in the scene in which he confesses his crime to Sonia: he begins by offering reasons, but she knows and he knows that they are not the true reasons, merely truth's public face. They must be gone through, put in words, offered as tokens of reality, so that they can eventually recede and take away with them all similarly ostensible reasons, leaving a void to be filled by the real truth, the exorbitance of Raskolnikov's will. Of such a hero we say that only his will fills the void it has caused. If he commits a crime, the crime is sustained only by the nature of the criminal will: causes drawn from his context are merely provisional – and the more plausible, the more provisional. Ahab and Raskolnikov are Prometheans because they strike through whatever conditions are offered them in the guise of reality: personal relationships, home, whaling, the ship, occupations. Such things merely thwart, and vainly, a reality known by the only admissible evidence, the pressure of feeling. Hence the great theme of such novels: the frightful violence of feeling for which no occasion can be found, the anarchy of feeling which can find no fulfilment in the available orthodox forms. In such a predicament, excess may run in either direction; to the saintly evacuation of self, as in Myshkin in *The Idiot*, or to the exorbitance of self, as in Raskolnikov. The two excesses know each other: thus Ahab speaks to Pip, as Lear to the Fool.

Raskolnikov glosses this predicament in Nietzschean terms, reciting the distinction between common and extraordinary men as meaning a corresponding distinction between two moralities, though he tells Porfiry that the welfare of mankind is the real justification of seemingly immoral acts. Present crimes are justified by future blessings. Raskolnikov says that the extraordinary man, the hero of his time, is he who 'speaks a new word'; presumably because the received language is merely 'last year's words', testifying to feelings already obsolete. But Dostoevsky does not let his hero run away with the novel as Melville nearly let Ahab run away with *Moby-Dick*: the distinction between common and extraordinary people is qualified and critically transformed by setting Sonia in relation to Raskolnikov. Sonia becomes everything by being nothing: in her own claimed right, that is, she is nothing, but in the reverberation of her meaning she becomes everything, she fills the void by not willing to fill anything. Against the new word which the Promethean hero claims to speak, there is the old word always new, the perennial language which Sonia does not speak in her own right but merely recites in her given voice from the story of the raising of Lazarus from the dead. Dostoevsky says of Raskolnikov: 'mere existence had never been enough for him; he had always wanted something more'.[1] When Raskolnikov falls ill, it is always from wounded pride, a sickness of the humiliated spirit, whatever physical form it takes. He is a criminal because he cannot find any institution, any form, willing to receive his feeling: instead of infusing his own life into clay, he kills the life which excludes him. Set against him, Sonia – like Ishmael in this respect – is one of those to whom everything is real and mere existence is enough: enough, because within that existence it is possible to love and to serve. If she is great in any respect, it is in the degree of her patience: even when she is baffled by circumstances, she never complains of their circumstantiality, she never frets against life. She is not one of those who are 'only moved' and have in themselves 'no source of movement', the source of movement is her love, her patience, her sense of the end-lessness of human and spiritual relations.

As for Dostoevsky himself in his ordering of the fiction: it is customary to emphasize his care for the errancy of his heroes, his running beside them into extremity, his profound sense of the 'chthonic powers' undermining the ground of orthodoxy. It is a custom no less honoured to emphasize the critical pressure he exerts upon Promethean aspirations, that 'he expressly condemns them, and prophesies their failure'. 'In his eyes,' Girard says, 'Nietzsche's superhumanity would have been merely an under-ground dream.'[2] In *Crime and Punishment* Dostoevsky goes to some lengths to redeem Raskolnikov, mainly through Sonia's mediation and the idiom of resurrection. Of the relation achieved between them he says: 'the heart of one held inexhaustible sources of life for the heart of the other.' At the end of the story he places upon such words as 'life' and 'love' burdens which they can hardly bear, even with Sonia's accepted history to sustain them. And he comes close to repudiating the Promethean experience altogether in Raskolnikov's last dream, where people run mad and none more desperately than those 'endowed with reason and will':

---

[1] Dostoevsky, *Crime and Punishment*, tr. David Magarshack. Harmondsworth. Penguin Books, 1951, p. 552.

[2] Girard, *supra*, p. 279.

> But these creatures were spirits endowed with reason and will. People who became infected with them at once became mad and violent. But never had people considered themselves as wise and as strong in their pursuit of truth as these plague-ridden people . . . Each of them believed that the truth only resided in him, and was miserable looking at the others, and smote his breast, wept, and wrung his hands.[1]

This comes on nearly the last page of the book, and it has an air of throwing everything into the scale on one side for fear the score may be settled by the other. Besides, motives once imaginatively grasped can hardly be let go, least of all by asserting that they have been let go. It is difficult to say, when we have come up to the last pages, whether or not their effect is more beautiful than perfunctory. They merely point to a resolution as if 'in our next', they do not go beyond an indication that Raskolnikov must be content to feel with Sonia's feeling for a long time before he can feel with his own, and that this accepted limitation may be the new form of his heroism. Perhaps it is enough. Dostoevsky does not choose to show, or else he has not been able to find dramatic images to represent, the new life which is to unfold; the New Testament and the story of Lazarus are as far as he goes in that way. Certainly, the Promethean aspirations are rebuked, if only by the implication that, outside the fiction, we could not tolerate them or provide an institutional order to contain them, short of a prison or a psychiatric hospital. Within the fiction, of course, it is another story, and those aspirations are irrefutable if for no other reason than that they have made nearly all the running. They are the action to which society can only respond with a reaction as bewildered as the original action was frightful. It is the wonderful old story, in which a writer's imagination conspires with the creatures it has created, and cannot help itself so long as the fiction persists. Dostoevsky is the novelist who takes special care of those who are never satisfied, even though he says to them at last: be satisfied. He has a particular feeling not for local dissatisfactions but for the aboriginal dissatisfaction which by definition can never be eased, short of death; the dissatisfaction of being human, of having a will

---

[1] *Crime and Punishment*, p. 555.

that cannot be fulfilled except by inventing monstrous forms of fulfilment. So there is always a circular movement, almost a tautology, in the history of such wills, and their release is merely one point along the circumference of their predicament. They cannot be satisfied by anything available to them, so they invent a form of action or an object of action; but the deed itself, willy-nilly, restores them to a common world and is never what they meant it to be. Dostoevsky's most avowed criticism of Promethean aspirations is not to show them absurd or inevitably defeated but to show them humiliated by their own futility: they were meant to be different in kind and they have turned out to be different only in theory. Raskolnikov discovers that his deed does not mean what he meant it to mean, it is merely one of many interchangeable forms of himself.

In Melville, the proportions of feeling are different. Of the amenity and plenitude of ordinary life he has as vivid a sense as he needs to have, though he stops far short of grounding supreme values upon that felicity. At one point Ahab says of himself:

> This lovely light, it lights not me; all loveliness is anguish to me, since I can ne'er enjoy. Gifted with the high perception, I lack the low, enjoying power; damned, most subtly and most malignantly! damned in the midst of Paradise![1]

If we can detach this from the Satan of *Paradise Lost*, we can find Melville's low, enjoying power at work in many chapters, especially in the chapter called 'A Squeeze of the Hand', the passage which Bachelard quoted to illustrate the poetry of touch;[2] as Ishmael describes squeezing the lumps of sperm back into fluid, he reaches a vertigo of ease and responsiveness totally freed from the venom of desire. I have heard this passage described as ironic, one of Melville's comic fancies culminating in the figment of angels in Paradise, 'each with his hands in a jar of spermaceti'. If the reader insists on taking it in this way, Melville's prose does not prevent it: the feeling of sensual music is compatible with a smiling

---

[1] *Moby-Dick*, p. 165.
[2] Gaston Bachelard, *La Terre et les reveries de la volonté*. Paris. Corti, 1948, pp. 80–4.

reflection upon its excess. But the passage still stands for all the other registered pleasures, equally provisional, but supremely good while they are allowed to last. Melville has this power among others, but it is not his special gift. His special gift is for the representation of motives so concentrated that they become one motive, and everything else pales in the light of the comparison. He is ready to start with diversity, but his characteristic talent forces its forms to transpire in one form. Faced with several motives or passions, he tends to require that they all assimilate themselves to one, a ruling passion, and if necessary suppress themselves so that one force may prevail. He lets his passions drive 'beyond good and evil' to a form of unity in which whatever is not assimilated is overwhelmed. In *Moby-Dick* with reference to Ahab he calls it 'monomania', but he could just as well have called it a ruling passion or a humour. Under whatever name, it is sponsored by his imagination as the characteristic form of his fiction: one character, increasingly identified with his will, concentrated in nature as in purpose, separates himself from the common world and keeps that separation to the end of the line. The figure runs all the way from Ahab to his fictive counterpart, Bartleby. Melville's relation to his time depends upon that form of his fiction, because it touches there the nineteenth century's preoccupation with the question of energy. Henry Adams's meditation on the dynamo as the modern form of force is only one example of many, but it is enough; his feeling of awe and bewilderment before that force is his century's form of caring, so far as it cared. Adams knew that the modern energies were more than men needed, and far more than they showed any sign of controlling or understanding. When he looked back to the thirteenth century he saw, or thought he saw, men supposing mind to be 'a mode of force directly derived from the intelligent prime motor, and the cause of all form and sequence in the universe'.[1] This is sometimes written off as Adams's New England nostalgia, but I take it as the form of his care, not about the thirteenth century but about the nineteenth and now the

---

[1] Henry Adams, *The Education of Henry Adams*. Boston. Houghton Mifflin, 1961, p. 429.

twentieth, the question of available force and its relation, if it can still have a relation, to men. We can be a little more specific. I am supposing a ground of common concern between the Melville of *Moby-Dick* and the Adams who said that 'energy is the inherent effort of every multiplicity to become unity'. And the question between them turns on the nature of that unity: does it retain the character of its origin, or does it destroy most of that character in the creation of unity as a second self, a demon? It is Yeats's question in 'Leda and the Swan', but turned askew, the question of a relation between power and knowledge, force and mind, will and order.

We can see now why Melville needed Starbuck and why Starbuck could not be enough. He needed him to keep before our minds the ball and chain of ordinary life, duties, occupations; and the sensual music of that life, too, its momentary accords. He needed Ishmael for a harder purpose. Ishmael speaks for the first person, the middle range of experience, good and bad, he exerts whatever force he has to keep the book from flying away or tearing itself apart. He sees limits with 'the equal eye'. Finally, he survives, because he must, not because he has charge of the story but because he has charge of ordinary life. But he is not enough, and the narrative must often be taken out of his hands or out of his voice. Some readers think that Melville was incompetent in this respect, setting Ishmael up as the narrative witness and then insinuating into his testimony things which he could not possibly have seen or heard; Ahab's soliloquies, and so forth. But the real narrator is the language, and Melville has Biblical authority for using finite witnesses and then, on high occasion, going beyond them to speak through their voices. It is the language which understands, what Ishmael merely feels without understanding, the energies run wild or run mad in the creation of the second self. Ishmael merely understands that there are forces at large somehow commensurate with the wilfulness of the sea and the whale: he cries out when he feels them, but he cannot name them or control them. The language can name them, because it has all the experience in the world in its veins, it has *King Lear* and the Bible and all the other experiences which first persons, at home to themselves, have no need of and cannot use. The language does the work which in James's fiction is done by fine intelligences registering the events, it reports the events and vouches for them on authority we can respect: but Melville's language has to do more than that, it has to see and feel and remember all round the subject, so that nothing in the case escapes from the language. To do so much, it must know nearly everything and feel nearly everything; whatever it fails in, it must not fail in sympathy.

But it must draw the line somewhere, if only because novels have to end, and having ended they must give the reader an impression of unity and coherence. One of the problems of the Promethean imagination is that it never knows exactly how to bring things to an end. There is nearly always, as I have remarked, a strain between the story and its moral. According to its moral, the myth of Prometheus is bound to be a cautionary tale: Prometheus was lucky to be reconciled to Zeus, after such a bout of defiance, and a hint of blasphemy. But the story, especially in its modern forms, goes as far as it can to withhold the moral, by presenting the high Promethean aspirations as intrinsically valid, if for no other reason than that they are exciting, they speak to many ordinary people of feelings just barely concealed. So the moral imposes an official answer, but it leaves the real question in the air. *Moby-Dick* is a cautionary tale, too, if we attend to Ishmael and take his prudent word for it; or even if we attend to Solomon, when Ishmael quotes him: 'The man that wandereth out of the way of understanding shall remain in the congregation of the dead'.[1] And Ishmael goes on:

> Give not thyself up, then, to fire, lest it invert thee, deaden thee; as for the time it did me. There is a wisdom that is woe; but there is a woe that is madness.[2]

'For the time'; the qualification is important. How we take this passage depends upon our sense of the story up to this point, and our sense of the language as perhaps qualifying that first sense, the extent to which we have gone along with its rhetoric. But this much may be said, that the aspiring language, the language in

---

[1] *Moby-Dick*, p. 422.   [2] *Ibid.*, pp. 422–3.

sympathy with Ahab's will, does not encourage us to rest without further ado in Solomon's wisdom. The language tempts us to believe that only by wandering out of the way of common understanding can we see and apprehend the white whale, and touch a wisdom more profound than prudence; and if that wandering consigns us to the congregation of the dead, well and good. 'Prudence is a rich, ugly old maid courted by Incapacity.' When a Promethean rhetoric is in full voice, this is what it says, it sets up a perspective in which common things appear insipid, and credences of summer a vulgar delusion.

There is a scene in *The Possessed* which touches upon this question, the penultimate chapter in which Stepan Verkhovensky is dying and he asks Mrs. Ulitin to read him something. She reads a passage from Revelation, the letter to the angel of the church in Laodicea:

> These things saith the Amen, the faithful and true witness, the beginning of the creation of God: I know thy works, that thou art neither cold nor hot: I would thou wert cold or hot. So because thou art lukewarm, and neither hot nor cold, I will spew thee out of my mouth.[1]

Verkhovensky seizes upon the text: 'You hear, better be cold than lukewarm, than *only* lukewarm!' And he calls for another reading, this time St. Luke's story of the man possessed by devils:

> And Jesus asked him, What is thy name? And he said, Legion; for many devils were entered into him. And they intreated him that he would not command them to depart into the abyss. Now there was there a herd of many swine feeding on the mountain: and they intreated him that he would give them leave to enter into them. And he gave them leave. And the devils came out from the man, and entered into the swine: and the herd rushed down the steep into the lake, and were choked.[2]

Verkhovensky applies the story to his own case in a way that need not concern us here. It is enough for our purpose if we say that the Promethean imagination goes all the way from the Laodiceans to

---

[1] Revelation 3.14–6. Cf. Dostoevsky, *The Devils* (*The Possessed*), tr. David Magarshack. Harmondsworth. Penguin Books, 1953, p. 646.

[2] St. Luke 8.30–3.

the lake in which the swine are choked. In the question of energy the Laodiceans are the force of inertia, the force by which matter tends, when at rest, to remain so, and, when in motion, to move only in a straight line. It is the force of 'our clayey part', without will or animation, and the Promethean imagination scorns it, since it has only the force of indifference. So the imagination runs away from it and determines to run not at all in a straight line but in a line according to its own will, straight or crooked. This is the beginning of the drama of consciousness, and one cannot be surprised if at times it looks like the work of the devil. At all events it begins in refusal, defiance, theft, blasphemy, all of these powered by pride and issuing in action. Thereafter the story is a dare-devil tale, and how it ends is our theme, variously negotiated in modern literature between such writers as Dostoevsky, Nietzsche, Melville, Rilke, and Mann, to name only a few in which the theme is palpable. It may appear melodramatic to fancy that it ends with the man possessed by devils, a Promethean in the direst straits, but how else could the man have got that way? When he cries out to be released, he is in the condition of Raskolnikov weeping before Sonia, having come to that Siberia of the spirit in which defiance has reached the end of its tether. There must either be a new life or an old life renewed; a new word, or an old word renewed.

Melville's image for this is the Catskill eagle:

> And there is a Catskill eagle in some souls that can alike dive down into the blackest gorges, and soar out of them again and become invisible in the sunny spaces. And even if he for ever flies within the gorge, that gorge is in the mountains; so that even in his lowest swoop the mountain eagle is still higher than other birds upon the plain, even though they soar.[1]

The air in Melville is the feminine element, the sea being masculine, equivalences given in the chapter called 'The Symphony'. So if the Catskill eagle is sustained by the air, while still exercising his freedom, the image is as tense and complete as Melville can make it, without direct recourse to its counterpart in personal relations; like the relation between Raskolnikov and Sonia. The image makes

---

[1] *Moby-Dick*, p. 423.

no concession to the ordinary world in terms of content, the eagle's experience ranges all the way between the blackest gorges and the sunny spaces. Of the four elements it eludes three, earth, fire, and water, but it exhibits in its chosen fourth that exact congruence of feeling and form which is, almost by default, Melville's theme.

Prometheus in Straits

IN the chapter of *The Rainbow* called 'The Man's World' Ursula Brangwen leaves home and goes to a teaching job in Nottingham. One of her colleagues, Maggie Schofield, is a suffragette, and they discuss the great questions, liberty, the place of women in the governing scheme of things. Maggie's desires are specific, and most of them may be fulfilled in the vote. But Lawrence says of Ursula in this chapter:

> She was in revolt. For once she were free she could get somewhere. Ah, the wonderful, real somewhere that was beyond her, the somewhere that she felt deep, deep inside her.
>
> In coming out and earning her own living she had made a strong, cruel move towards freeing herself. But having more freedom she only became more profoundly aware of the big want. She wanted so many things. She wanted to read great, beautiful books, and be rich with them; she wanted to see beautiful things, and have the joy of them for ever; she wanted to know big, free people; and there remained always the want she could put no name to.[1]

Lawrence's fiction, it will readily be agreed, depends upon the drama of specific desires: his characters are invariably articulate in naming them and pursuing them. They are finite people and they have finite objects, for the most part, in view. But it may also be said of Lawrence that he is peculiarly responsive to nameless desires, to states of desire which are not fulfilled or exhausted by anything specifically achieved. There is always a further radiance beyond the radiance of any single object attained. Lawrence's fiction is Promethean in the sense that its demands are endless, his art is most deeply engaged when the action is propelled by desire, and the desire goes beyond anything that can be named. His typical characters, those we think of as sustaining most of the burdens of his fiction, are restless, never satisfied, they live on the nerves of demand: when they are not restless, we feel that they are in abeyance. Just as their lives are exacerbated by possibilities felt beyond anything actual, so too the language of their fiction is always straining beyond itself, as if it thought its greatest effects merely banal by comparison with sublime effects in the silence beyond words. It is only a minor exaggeration to say that Lawrence's words are never satisfied

---

[1] D. H. Lawrence, *The Rainbow*. Harmondsworth. Penguin Books, 1949, p. 406.

with themselves, they want to be finer than their best selves, and strain as if answering appeals or imprecations across a void, often at the cost of falling below their ordinary powers. R. P. Blackmur said of Lawrence's language in the poems that it was 'commonplace for everything except its intensity',[1] and if we want to take the harm out of the comment we can say that the language would be commonplace but for one saving grace, whether the grace is intensity or some other quality. Much of Lawrence's writing is like his own description of Etruscan vases, 'the naturalness', he says, 'verging on the commonplace, but usually missing it'.[2] It is as if the commonplace were always present in Lawrence's writing, either as substance or as accident, but mostly as something to be transcended. I take it as standing for specific desires and particular effects, and it plays its part in naming the specific things, so that Lawrence's spirit may rush beyond them. This is a feature of his art, which we call restlessness when it inhabits his characters. It is an art which arises from inordinate demands upon life, and what it comes to is an insistence that life be transfigured in the art; nothing less could answer. The relation between Lawrence and his art is therefore only a special case of his relation to life itself, and both relations are like Will Brangwen's relation to his child Ursula:

> Her father was the dawn wherein her consciousness woke up. But for him, she might have gone on like the other children, Gudrun and Theresa and Catherine, one with the flowers and insects and playthings, having no existence apart from the concrete object of her attention. But her father came too near to her. The clasp of his hands and the power of his breast woke her up almost in pain from the transient unconsciousness of childhood. Wide-eyed, unseeing, she was awake before she knew how to see.[3]

Lawrence's relation to life was similarly inordinate, out of season. He quarrelled with life not because it refused to admit desire but because it would not tolerate the endlessness of desire. He quar-

---

[1] R. P. Blackmur, *Form and Value in Modern Poetry*. New York. Doubleday Anchor Books, 1957, p. 261.

[2] D. H. Lawrence, *Mornings in Mexico, and Etruscan Places*. Harmondsworth. Penguin Books, 1960, p. 130.

[3] *The Rainbow*, p. 221.

relled with the available forms of fiction because, doing so much, they did not do everything. He scorned the specific things they provided, out of desire for the nameless things they would not even try to name. In *Sons and Lovers* when Miriam would ask Paul, of one of his sketches, 'Why do I like this so?', Paul would say that it was as if he had painted 'the shimmering protoplasm in the leaves and everywhere, and not the stiffness of the shape'. 'Only this shimmeriness is the real living', he would say, 'The shape is a dead crust'.[1] Lawrence associated the available forms of fiction with the dead crust, and with what in a famous letter to Edward Garnett he calls 'the old stable *ego* – of the character'.[2] Under any of these guises, the complaint is the same. Lawrence is restless with the forms that life has taken, he wants to transcend them or go beneath them to the protoplasm still innocent of form and shape. A reader of *Sons and Lovers* is inclined to ask: what promise did God ever give Paul Morel that He would make an exception in his favour or redeem him alone from the fate of being finite?

The myth of Prometheus answers to this pattern of feeling when it is interpreted as testifying to the endlessness and the namelessness of man's desires. Even when desires are named, they retain their mark of ultimacy, scorning whatever is merely local or provisional. When the story was translated into Christian terms, it featured, as in Tertullian and Ficino, the struggle of the soul to achieve complete truth, a condition beyond the sum of finite revelations.[3] In Lawrence, the characteristic movement of feeling is from finite satisfactions to a corresponding distress, and the deepest distress arises from the realization that the satisfactions are merely finite. One of the marks of his fiction is that it registers the nameless desire by surrounding it with the most acute approximations: the real object of desire is what the approximations miss. Lawrence's

---

[1] D. H. Lawrence, *Sons and Lovers*. London. Heinemann, 1956, p. 152.

[2] D. H. Lawrence, *Collected Letters*, edited by Harry T. Moore. London. Heinemann, 1962, Vol. I, p. 282. Letter of June 5, 1914.

[3] Tertullian, 'Adversus Marcionem', *Patrologiae Latinae*, ed. Migne (Paris 1844–1903), p. 271. Ficino, 'Argumentum in Protagoram', *Opera*, 1576, Vol. II, p. 1298. Cited in Olga Raggio, 'The Myth of Prometheus', *Journal of the Warburg Institute*, Vol. XXI (1958), pp. 44–62.

Prometheanism is the hyperbole of feeling, subject to the qualification that its desires cannot be registered by any figures of speech. In *The Rainbow* Ursula feels, after an episode of intercourse with Skrebensky, that 'it was as if she had received another nature. She belonged to the eternal, changeless place into which they had leapt together',[1] but ten pages later she knows that she has not received another nature, but only the humiliation of her own. It would take a second nature to satisfy the demands of the first, except that the second would require a third, and so on to whatever nature is accomplished in death. Visionary rainbows are as provisional as anything else.

Perhaps this accounts for Lawrence's special feeling for that chapter in *The Return of the Native* where Hardy describes the bonfires. Hardy writes:

> Moreover to light a fire is the instinctive and resistant act of man when, at the winter ingress, the curfew is sounded throughout Nature. It indicates a spontaneous, Promethean rebelliousness against the fiat that this recurrent season shall bring foul times, cold darkness, misery and death. Black chaos comes, and the fettered gods of the earth say, Let there be light.[2]

In the nature of the case, a bonfire is a hopeless gesture, a doomed synecdoche, the desperate face of festivity, revealed when the holiday is over. Hardy respects it for that reason, he is as tenderly disposed to the bonfire-makers as Lawrence to the victims of nameless desires. In each case, the feeling cannot be fulfilled in fact; fact merely drives the feeling to further exorbitance. So it is easy to see why Lawrence's happiest symbol is the phoenix, *unica semper avis*, and why the phoenix is a euphemism, as near as Lawrence ever comes to naming his ultimate desire. It may be said that the phoenix is a hopeless gesture, and beloved for that reason; the only necessary qualification to go with that statement is that we are conceived in such conceits. It is this conceit which enables Mellors, in the letter to Connie which brings *Lady Chatterley's Lover* to an end, to say on one page that 'there's a bad time coming', and

---

[1] *The Rainbow*, p. 451.

[2] Thomas Hardy, *The Return of the Native*. London, Macmillan, 1965 reprint, p. 23.

nevertheless to say on the next, 'I believe in the little flame between us'.[1] The little flame is passion, the flame in which the phoenix is reborn.

To describe Lawrence's characteristic feeling as restlessness is merely another approximation. To come nearer to it, I might say that it is Will Brangwen's feeling in the 'Anna Victrix' chapter when, having acknowledged that he lives only for Anna and the children, he says that there is something more:

> He was attended by a sense of something more, something further, which gave him absolute being. It was as if now he existed in Eternity, let Time be what it might.[2]

But he is still unsure. And his feeling is answered by Anna's, even in her victory:

> She was straining her eyes to something beyond. . . . Something she had not, something she did not grasp, could not arrive at. . . . In the winter, when she rose with the sunrise, and out of the back windows saw the east flaming yellow and orange above the green, glowing grass, while the great pear-tree in between stood dark and magnificent as an idol, and under the dark pear-tree, the little sheet of water spread smooth in burnished, yellow light, she said, 'It is here'. And when, at evening, the sunset came in a red glare through the big opening in the clouds, she said again, 'It is beyond'.[3]

Another form the feeling takes is that of Gerald's will in *Women in Love*, his desire to control the resistant Matter of the earth, the desire, as Lawrence says, 'for a perfect intervening mechanism between man and Matter, the desire to translate the Godhead into pure mechanism'.[4] In that determination, the efficiency which Gerald imposes on the coal-mine is merely a note toward his supreme fiction, the ultimate conquest of matter by will. The machine is his means, but only because it is the instrument of his will. Since machines and coal-mines are specific, they are not in

---

[1] D. H. Lawrence, *Lady Chatterley's Lover*. Harmondsworth. Penguin Books, 1960, pp. 315, 316.

[2] *The Rainbow*, pp. 193–4.

[3] *Ibid.*, p. 195.

[4] D. H. Lawrence, *Women in Love*. Harmondsworth. Penguin Books, 1960, p. 257.

truth the sufficient objects of Gerald's desire, but merely its provisional occasions. We register the feeling most powerfully when what we are offered to account for it or to assuage it is merely an excuse or a delusion; the truth is somewhere beyond. We feel it in the strain of the language, when like Desdemona we understand a fury in the words, but not the words. It was Tolstoy and not Lawrence who said, 'God is the name of my desire', but it is Lawrence's words that make us feel that nothing less than a theology of desire would do, a revelation in words for which the actual words on the page are mere tokens in passing.

I am arguing that the essential feeling in Lawrence, the feeling which makes us think of its approximate marks as typically Lawrentian, is a profound spiritual restlessness, a Promethean urge to transfigure life by driving it beyond itself. We have grown accustomed to this feeling, we think we can almost anticipate it. So the most memorable and astonishing moments in Lawrence's fiction are those in which an impatient man is, for once, patient, and sits still. Nothing is more remarkable in Tom Brangwen than the patience, the quiet confidence, with which he waits upon his fate, and recognizes it in Lydia Lensky when she comes. 'It was coming, he knew, his fate. The world was submitting to its transformation. He made no move: it would come, what would come'.[1] What is incalculable in that passage is that the idiom is Promethean, the world submitting to its transformation, but precisely the opposite force is at work, too, the patience, the waiting. It is the same patience which Tom declares in the consummate scene where he brings little Anna out to the barn, at night, feeding the cows, while her mother is in labour. There is an essential stillness at the heart of Tom's violence. As the generations follow one another, the difficulty of this stillness increases, though enough of it remains to allow Ursula, in the scene in which she gives her necklace to the child on the barge, to feel that there are possibilities which the mere plot of her present life humiliates: Skrebensky is alien to those possibilities in one way, she herself in another. But the barge-man is not refuted. These possibilities are featured again

---

[1] *The Rainbow*, p. 32.

in Lawrence's story 'The Blind Man', where Maurice Pervin's contact with the world, his certainty of touch, gives him patience, and the power of patience. The fiction does not swing equably between restlessness and rest, it is whirled from one extreme to the other, and these terms are its coordinates. Lawrence is always ready to name a force, distinguish between its rival kinds, with an implication that, beyond all the finite kinds, there is something else, a meta-force with no name. There is something of this in the second version of *Lady Chatterley's Lover*, where Connie thinks of energy:

> She realised there were two main sorts of energy, the frictional, seething, resistant, explosive, blind sort, like that of steam-engines and motor-cars and electricity, and of people such as Clifford and Bill Tewson and modern, insistent women, and these queer vacuous miners: then there was the other, forest energy, that was still and softly powerful, with tender, frail bud-tips and gentle finger-ends full of awareness.[1]

The fact that the first kind is given with its human equivalents, and the second only in organic or botanical terms makes it plain that the search for the human equivalent of that forest energy is one of Lawrence's own preoccupations. If life is to be transformed, its new form must correspond to the forest, but up to now it has no name, only its enemy has a name. Wallace Stevens has a poem, 'The River of Rivers in Connecticut', in which he says of that river that 'It is not to be seen beneath the appearances / That tell of it'. Lawrence's fiction is nervous and restless because it feels itself dispossessed of power which can be felt but not possessed in the appearances that tell of it: what the appearances tell is that it is beyond them.

Or beneath them: that is another possibility, in an area of concern marked out by botany, anthropology, and archaeology. Lawrence's fiction, in which dissatisfaction and friction are so often the substance, is sustained by a pastoral myth of the liaison between man and nature. If we think of it as animated by forest energy, we guard ourselves against misinterpreting it as a quietist dream, a sinking to rest in the 'green world' of original Nature. In *Etruscan Places* Lawrence says that 'the old religion of the profound attempt

---

[1] D. H. Lawrence, *John Thomas and Lady Jane*. London. Heinemann, 1972, p. 367.

of man to harmonize himself with nature, and hold his own and come to flower in the great seething of life, changed with the Greeks and Romans into a desire to resist nature, to produce a mental cunning and a mechanical force that would outwit Nature and chain her down completely, completely, till at last there should be nothing free in nature at all, all should be controlled, domesticated, put to man's meaner uses'.[1] The Nature which Lawrence invokes is passionate rather than picturesque, it is propelled by such forces as those represented by the horse St. Mawr in 'a world beyond our world',[2] forces which even yet one could imagine oneself worshipping, propitiating, acknowledging. Such a world is simple only in the sense of elemental; a temple for worship, not a place to rest. Lawrence accepts the reading of the Prometheus myth in which the harmony of man and Nature is disturbed by the theft of knowledge in the form of fire: the harmony is broken, for good and ill. Sometimes he hates consciousness for the division it has caused between body and spirit. Sometimes he celebrates it for the intensity, including the intensity of anguish, which it makes possible. But the novels are attempts to drive beyond consciousness to a new unity, a second pastoral made possible by the fortunate or dreadful fall of man. We must come, either for the first or second time, into what Will Brangwen calls 'the land of intimate connexion'.[3] In *The Rainbow*, as in the other major novels, this drive beyond consciousness is ascribed mainly to the women, especially to Anna and Ursula. The presence of knowledge, in the Promethean history of man, is taken for granted; there is no presented urge to disown it, except fancifully in the verbal game between Ursula and Birkin when Ursula wants the world to start all over again, 'a new start, non-human',[4] or fancifully again in *St. Mawr*, the speculations about a clean world prior to man. Generally, the historical fact of consciousness is taken for granted, and the problem is to repair its defects or transfigure its standard forms. Lawrence's heroines aspire

---

[1] *Mornings in Mexico, and Etruscan Places*, p. 174.

[2] D. H. Lawrence, *St. Mawr, and The Virgin and the Gipsy*. Harmondsworth. Penguin Books, 1950, p. 34.

[3] *The Rainbow*, p. 151.   [4] *Women in Love*, p. 142.

beyond consciousness, but their aspirations are never fulfilled in fact. The men do not try so often or so hard, they are closer to nature, the women closer to culture. The risk is taken mostly by the women, and they bear the appalling wounds, the fracture of personality, when they mistake their own will for the creative force at large. It is not Skrebensky who is ruined, but Ursula. Skrebensky is overwhelmed by Ursula, diminished by her will, but he was never really more than he is now, and he is not worth ruining: so he recovers as much as he needs to recover to marry a Colonel's daughter and live the life of a cavalry officer in India. Ursula is ruined, so far as *The Rainbow* goes, she ruins herself by claiming the infinite as her portion. What Ursula wants is what Lawrence wants, the triumph of a new life over the old divisions of consciousness and ego; a new form of unity which corresponds to the imagination as distinct from reason; the one, creative, where the other is mechanical.

Clearly, Lawrence's imagination could not be content with rest or the mere lapse of energy or desire, as if the drive beyond consciousness were merely abandoned. It would have to be the kind of rest that comes after restlessness and retains the sign of its origin. When Lawrence was working on the novel which eventually became *The Rainbow* and *Women in Love*, he wrote to Henry Savage, telling him that the new work was very different from *Sons and Lovers*:

> The Laocoön writhing and shrieking have gone from my new work, and I think there is a bit of stillness, like the wide, still, unseeing eyes of a Venus of Melos. . . . There is something in the Greek sculpture that any soul is hungry for – something of the eternal stillness that lies under all movement, under all life, like a source, incorruptible and inexhaustible. It is deeper than change, and struggling. So long I have acknowledged only the struggle, the stream, the change. And now I begin to feel something of the source, the great impersonal which never changes and out of which all change comes.[1]

The writhing and shrieking had not, indeed, finally gone from Lawrence's work, but the major novels have at least an intermittent and powerful sense of the source at rest. Even when he is speaking

---

[1] *Collected Letters*, Vol. I, p. 241. Letter of ? Autumn 1913.

of the war between mental consciousness and blood-consciousness, he retains a feeling for the impersonal source beyond consciousness. Again, whatever is of two kinds contains the possibility of coming in a third kind, transcending the divisions of the two. A work writhes and shrieks when it has only a sense of the appalling division, and no sense of the unity before or after. The parable of unity is recited in the New England woman's story in *St. Mawr*, where Lawrence describes the two worlds she sees, the hard immediate world when she keeps her eyes near the ground, and the other world when she looks far into the distance:

> So it was when you watched the vast and living landscape. The landscape lived, and lived as the world of the gods, unsullied and unconcerned. The great circling landscape lived its own life, sumptuous and uncaring. Man did not exist for it.
>
> And if it had been a question simply of living through the eyes, into the *distance*, then this would have been Paradise, and the little New England woman on her ranch would have found what she was always looking for, the earthly paradise of the spirit.
>
> But even a woman cannot live only into the distance, the beyond. Willy-nilly she finds herself juxtaposed to the near things, the thing in itself. And willy-nilly she is caught up into the fight with the immediate object.[1]

What Lawrence himself saw in the distance is his pastoral of forest energy, the vitality of plants, animals, and fish, the Etruscan religion, Indian dances and rituals, the flow of mystery beneath its appearances. What he saw, caught up into the fight with the immediate object, need not be specified, it is omnivorous.

There is another way of putting this. Lawrence wants to go beyond or beneath the given world by restoring the magical sense of nature; or a new sense of nature corresponding to magic, except that it comes after the experience of a divisive consciousness and not before it. It is not a matter of putting back the clock, or, as Wyndham Lewis argued, adopting one of the available forms of primitivism. Magic is what Lawrence called 'the subjective control of the great natural powers',[2] as distinct from the objective or

---

[1] *St. Mawr, and the Virgin and the Gipsy*, p. 155.
[2] *Mornings in Mexico, and Etruscan Places*, p. 173.

administrative power which he associated with the Romans: it goes along with 'the vitality of the cosmos, the myriad vitalities in wild confusion, which still is held in some sort of array: and man, amid all the glowing welter, adventuring, struggling, striving for one thing, life, vitality, more vitality: to get into himself more and more of the gleaming vitality of the cosmos'.[1] If we present Lawrence, then, as a great historical novelist, pointing to his sense of English life and society in the throes of change, we should go on to say that these powers, fine as they are, are only incidental. Lawrence is primarily concerned with the ghostly aspect of reality, the sense in which it is before and after history, and often confounding history.[2] Equally, when Lawrence preferred augury and divination to their modern versions, psychology and political science, the reason was that he preferred a live universe to a dead universe: the first supposes a universe in which men joined their powers with greater powers, the second supposes a universe in which men have nothing but themselves. In *Science and Poetry* I. A. Richards rebuked Lawrence, in effect, for this preference, for writing as if he might still prevent 'the Neutralization of Nature, the transference from the Magical View of the world to the scientific'.[3] Richards thought Lawrence merely perverse, indulging himself in fashionable primitivism, refusing to face up to 'those difficulties which come from being born into this generation rather than into some earlier age'.[4] But Lawrence was not beating an antique drum; nostalgia accounts for virtually nothing in his art. He was not proposing to go back to astrology and augury, but to effect a revolution, a radical change of heart, for which astrology and augury were the merest approximations. He does not write of

---

[1] *Ibid.*, pp. 147–8.

[2] Musil on *The Man Without Qualities*: 'I am not concerned with actual events. Events, anyhow, are interchangeable. I am interested . . . in what one might call the ghostly aspect of reality.' Quoted in Georg Lukacs, *The Meaning of Contemporary Realism*, translated by John and Necke Mander, London. Merlin Press, 1963, p. 25.

[3] I. A. Richards, *Science and Poetry*. London. Kegan Paul, Trench, Trubner, 1926, p. 47.

[4] *Ibid.*, p. 72.

the modern world as if it had never happened, but as if it had now to be transfigured. Such transfiguration would be impossible in a scientific world governed by mechanism and the divided consciousness.

In fact, Lawrence's major novels have one theme, the possibility of redeeming human relationships, so that they can participate in the great natural adventure of creation and imagination. Since Lawrence registers experience as 'the come-and-go of the life-powers',[1] his test for any human relationship is always: does it respond to the natural rhythm of flowing, change, and return? Does it exhibit such range and freedom that local restraints do not matter? This is the idiom Lawrence uses in the famous comment about the novel in *Lady Chatterley's Lover*:

> It can inform and lead into new places the flow of our sympathetic consciousness, and it can lead our sympathy away in recoil from things gone dead.[2]

So his terms of praise are words of movement, keeping life open for transfiguration: such words as quick, wonder, fresh, spontaneous, vital, life, bold, natural, free, wild, dangerous, flowing, touch. And the hated terms are: convention, friction, mentality, mechanism, furtive, mean, stale, and any other terms which presuppose a formula already imposed upon life, and fixed in that determination. The possibility of transfiguration is now a human possibility, the natural adventure is handed over to men and women, they must transfigure themselves and each other if life itself is to be redeemed. So the major novels feature a new beginning, the men and women have to depend upon themselves and upon each other; though they live in a community and sometimes find operative values there, they cannot rely upon those values as source of their own lives. They cannot take their bearings from the society in which they live, even though occasional grace may reach them from that quarter. Especially in the later novels, Lawrence assumes that operative values in society are forces already lost, as lost as the world of *Under the Greenwood Tree*, and that serious life must start again with the individual. Sex is a

---

[1] *Mornings in Mexico, and Etruscan Places*, p. 207.
[2] *Lady Chatterley's Lover*, p. 104.

beginning again, in a society of two people, otherwise disinherited. Lawrence's heroes, and still more his heroines, confronted with the mechanically ordained conventions of society, try to clear a space for themselves by a prolonged effort of consciousness and interrogation. They make a bid for freedom in general by seeking their own freedom in particular. They try to produce the conditions in their own lives which we can only associate now with 'other worlds', wildernesses, deserts, or a planet just barely colonized. The object is to reach a condition of absolute fulfilment by way of local fulfilments, a Rananim of two people, to begin with. When Lawrence's heroes and heroines 'succeed', their success is visible only in themselves: eventually, it will make a difference to society, but such a positive conclusion is not Lawrence's story. If Birkin and Ursula have come through, their arrival is not shown as having any demonstrable effect upon a society, it is enough that they have succeeded by salient contrast with Gerald and Gudrun who have disastrously failed. Success and failure refer to changes in the coordinates of a relationship; failure tends to be more decisive than success. In the case of *Women in Love* Dr. Leavis has argued that 'in Birkin's married relations with Ursula the book invites us to localize the positive, the conceivable and due – if only with difficulty attainable – solution of the problem; the norm, in relation to which Gerald's disaster gets its full meaning'.[1] This seems to me false to the spirit of Lawrence's fiction. At the end of the novel, Birkin, in despair after Gerald's death, says to Ursula:

> Having you, I can live all my life without anybody else, any other sheer intimacy. But to make it complete, really happy, I wanted eternal union with a man too: another kind of love.

Ursula answers that this is 'an obstinacy, a theory, a perversity': 'you can't have two kinds of love. Why should you!' And the book ends with the quarrel about to begin. The reader's mind goes back at once to the scene, in the chapter called 'Man to Man',

---

[1] F. R. Leavis, *D. H. Lawrence, Novelist*. London. Chatto and Windus, 1967, p. 174.

in which Birkin asked Gerald to swear a bond of eternal love, and
the chapter called 'Gladiatorial' in which that love is released, if not
declared. So Birkin and Ursula have touched upon a radical matter,
and though we do not hear the quarrel, we know its nature. The
criticism is blunt, therefore, which speaks of the married relation
between Birkin and Ursula as the positive solution of the problem.
The quality of that relation is capable of debate, but it is impossible
to say of it that it presents the solution of any problem. I read the
last pages not separately from the enactment of the relationship up
to that point, but as bringing that relationship to a stage at which
Lawrence chooses to break off. The scene marks his attempt to
stave off the transformation of the lives of Birkin and Ursula into
destiny. Lawrence wants to show those lives as still moving in flux
and possibility. He prevents us from ascribing to them the finality
of definition. Strictly speaking, we cannot pronounce upon those
lives except grossly by contrasting them with those of Gudrun and
Gerald; or, with equal grossness, by listing their presented contents
– which would have to include, for Birkin, his traffic with deathli-
ness, his black river of dissolution, primal desire beyond love, *fleurs
du mal*, his demand that Ursula surrender her spirit to him, besides
extraordinary self-knowledge and delicacy; and, for Ursula, her
assertive will, her tyranny, her appalling modernity, as well as her
own kind of self-knowledge, her own kind of delicacy. The list
is of no account, because Lawrence consigns the significance of
these lives to the flow of their existence, not to achieved states or
definitions of being. The medium in which Birkin and Ursula live
is the free rise and fall of their feeling, the only name it bears is the
name of action. When we speak of the meaning of the relationship,
we do not refer to its pedagogical or exemplary bearing upon
society. Historical novelists write of society as if it were nature:
the detail of their writing corresponds to the minute descriptions
proffered by the natural historian. But Lawrence is not in that sense
a historical novelist, he does not believe that society is nature. In
his vision, nature is occluded by society, and the reality of nature
can only be felt, so far as characters in fiction are concerned,
through the gap between one psyche and another. Nature can be
registered most profoundly when the pressure of society is lifted,

and individual feeling flows between itself and its aboriginal source. That is why his heroes and heroines seem to live by conspiracy, forming cells, secret societies among themselves which start life all over again upon a secret compact between man and nature. In such conspiracies, the public structures of society are felt as obstacles, irritating or merely tedious. The only valuable life, according to Lawrence's fiction, is the individual adventure, a struggle toward new coordinates of being.

In the later fiction especially, these coordinates are sought in terms of man, woman, and the earth. The love between Connie and Mellors is registered as good when it is felt in league with the earth and the sun, the cycle of the seasons, the pause of winter before the spring of 'the drawing together'. The classic text for this phase of Lawrence's feeling is *St. Mawr*, where the dominant spirit is that the dead will have to bury their dead: as for the living, let them retreat to the desert, and fight. At least they must not yield to 'the bad time coming'. Life must begin again, starting from the earth. I associate this phase in Lawrence not only with apocalyptic literature generally but with a particular passage in Revelation (12: 16) which tells of the dragon. After the war in Heaven, when the red dragon is cast down upon the earth and sets about persecuting the woman arrayed with the sun, the woman is given the wings of an eagle, to escape. The dragon spews a river out of its mouth, hoping to catch the woman and drown her in it. But, according to Revelation, 'the earth helped the woman': it opened its mouth and swallowed the river which the dragon had cast forth. I take Lawrence's last fictions as parallel texts to this passage in Revelation, because if there is a discernible movement of feeling between *Women in Love* and *St. Mawr*, it is in the registered sense of the individual's retreat to the desert, and starting again. *Fantasia of the Unconscious* is Lawrence's handbook for this enterprise, and since it is based upon the human body rather than upon the nature of substance, it proposes a metabiology rather than a metaphysics.[1] *St. Mawr* represents a broken-hearted woman turning away from

---

[1] Cf. Kenneth Burke, *Permanence and Change*. Los Altos. Hermes Publications, 1954, p. 261.

the friction of human relationships to the world of forest energy. Lou Witt is to replace the old life of sexual relations with a new life in which equal intensity, but not equal exorbitance, will be lavished upon the relation between herself and her landscape; the wild spirit she feels at large in her New Mexican ranch. Meanwhile, as a preparation for that encounter, she must be 'very, very still' and recover her soul. In these last fictions, including *Lady Chatterley's Lover*, there is a determination on Lawrence's part to clear the decks, rid the world of its broken faith, and start again; by a cleansing violence, as in *Lady Chatterley's Lover*, or by a retreat to the desert, as in *St. Mawr*.

In either version, there is an implicit critique of the Promethean spirit, a critique which goes back to *The Rainbow*, to Ursula's letter to Skrebensky, where she accuses herself of arrogance and pride:

> But instead of thankfully, on my knees, taking what God had given, I must have the moon in my keeping, I must insist on having the moon for my own. Because I could not have it, everything else must go.[1]

Lawrence recognized in himself a Prometheus: he makes it clear in a letter to Bertrand Russell, February 12, 1915, that the current relation between himself and his experience in the world is understandable in Promethean terms.[2] But he interpreted the myth in terms of the incorrigible human ego: he speaks of man 'terribly suffering on the rock of his own egotism'.[3] Still, the question is bound to be ambiguous. Lawrence rebukes the will, but the rebuke is itself a function of the will. Again he posits two kinds of will, corresponding to the two kinds of energy, and sponsors that will which issues from forest energy. According to that preference, the individual will would preserve its purity by associating itself with the creative spirit of the world, content to participate in its work. The question is crucial in Lawrence's major fiction, since most of the quarrels between heroes and heroines turn upon bitter disagreements about the kind of will exhibited in each case. When they quarrel about love, they are really quarrelling about will, its nature, force, and direction. Lawrence is deeply implicated in these quarrels, as also in the Promethean history of man. That is why the charac-

---

[1] *The Rainbow*, p. 485.   [2] *Collected Letters*, Vol. I, p. 318.   [3] *Ibid.*, p. 301.

teristic rhythm of his scenes begins with restlessness or violence, exhausts itself and lapses into peace, and then either rises to the state of transfiguration or fastens again upon a minor tributary of dissatisfaction. In the great 'Moony' chapter of *Women in Love*, the violence begins with Birkin throwing dead flowers on the water, cursing Cybele, and stoning the moon's light. After each attack, the moon's light renews itself, the scattered fragments come together, and at last there is peace. At this stage Ursula comes upon the scene, she quarrels with Birkin about will and love and service; the quarrel subsides, they are at peace, in stillness. But there is no transfiguration. Alone, Birkin meditates upon two rival ways of experience, the African way, sensual, unspiritual, 'mindless progressive knowledge through the senses', and the other way, the 'paradisal entry into pure, single being, the individual soul taking precedence over love and desire for union, stronger than any pangs of emotion, a lovely state of free proud singleness, which accepted the obligation of the permanent connexion with others, and with the other, submits to the yoke and leash of love, but never forfeits its own proud individual singleness, even while it loves and yields'.[1] Immediately he rushes off to ask Ursula to marry him. But she does not answer, she knows that her will and his are not in accord. There is no transfiguration. The transfiguration comes only in the 'Excurse' chapter, in which the paradigm of restlessness, peace, and transfiguration is fully enacted. The peace is always tentative, good while it lasts, the transfiguration is rather a sudden gleam than a steady light, and most of the Lawrentian music is in the first movement, the restlessness. At least that is where his spirit comes to us, irresistibly.

The conclusion is that Lawrence was at once a true Promethean and an acute critic of the Promethean spirit in himself. He set the value of peace against the more spontaneous value of violence, and knew that both must be held in poise, if the work is to survive as something separable from the man who wrote it. This would be a happy conclusion, if it could be reached without softening the facts. But it can hardly be reached at all until we register the case

---

[1] *Women in Love*, p. 287.

against Lawrence. I am sure that many readers of Lawrence have had the experience of feeling, even while allowing his fiction to seize them, that it would be possible to hold themselves aloof. They could do this either by refusing Lawrence's coordinates altogether or by thinking them incomplete. Thus R. P. Blackmur resisted seizure by thinking Lawrence a terrible victim of the fallacy of 'expressive form', and his fiction ruined for lack of control. 'In D. H. Lawrence,' he argued, 'the hysteria of direct sensual experience destroys every structure of sensibility, and there is only as much human relation as there is possible in the swoon of the blood, which is a very powerful and very destructive relation indeed.'[1] I take this to mean that Lawrence never allowed the formal or rational imagination to intervene, while the experience provoked by the sensual imagination was in a rush, but only later, if at all, when the damage was already done. Or, in still other words, that he never wanted anything for his emotion but its completion. If these sentences mean anything, taken together, they refer to an element of insistence in Lawrence, which opens up a rift between the experience and its meaning. The rift, I think, is only intermittent; its sign, in Lawrence's style, is a certain theatricality, a relentlessness, a nagging habit of language. Thus a passage from the relation of Ursula and Skrebensky, in Nottingham, demands that we take Lawrence at his word, but the word is sustained by nothing but his will, which for the time being is merely a browbeating violence:

> He kissed her, with his soft, enveloping kisses, and she responded to them completely, her mind, her soul gone out. Darkness cleaving to darkness, she hung close to him, pressed herself into soft flow of his kiss, pressed herself down, down to the source and core of his kiss, herself covered and enveloped in the warm, fecund flow of his kiss, that travelled over her, flowed over her, covered her, flowed over the last fibre of her, so they were one stream, one dark fecundity, and she clung at the core of him, with her lips holding open the very bottommost source of him.[2]

---

[1] R. P. Blackmur, *Anni Mirabiles 1921–1925*. Washington. Library of Congress, 1956, p. 16.
[2] *The Rainbow*, pp. 446–7.

Lawrence is bullying the language, forcing 'dark' and 'fecund' to give up secrets we cannot really believe they possess. It is a terrible effect of such language that the more it is bullied the more sullen and inexpressive it becomes, and the more enraged the bully. E. M. Cioran says that if you take a word, repeat it several times, examine it, 'it will vanish, and in consequence something will vanish in you'.[1] What vanishes in Lawrence is his confidence, his sense of being in command of himself; what remains is a fanaticism of the will.

But we are all aware that the critical force which holds out against Lawrence, and makes the encounter a classic case in the reception of modern literature, is not Blackmur or Richards but Eliot. It is the juxtaposition of Lawrence and Eliot which demands from us the most sustained response, when we bring to mind not only Eliot's specific comments but the sense of life and the sense of literature which incited them. We have to take the strain of Eliot and Lawrence as presences, for our purpose, equal and opposite. The basic charge which Eliot brings against Lawrence is the charge which Chekhov brought against Dostoevksy: pretentiousness, spiritual immodesty, Eliot called it spiritual pride.[2] 'That dominating, cross-grained and extreme personality,' Eliot called him, 'a man of fitful and profound insights, rather than of ratiocinative powers; and therefore he was an impatient man.'[3] He was impatient, Eliot implied, because he thought that everything depended upon himself; or, in Blackmur's version, because he hardly ever 'saw the use of anything that did not immediately devour his interest, whether in life or in art'.[4] Eliot associated this charge with

---

[1] E. M. Cioran, *The Temptation to Exist*, translated by Richard Howard. Chicago. Quadrangle Books, 1968, p. 190.

[2] Eliot's review of John Middleton Murry's *Son of Woman* was published in *The Criterion*, Vol. X, No. 41, July 1931, pp. 768–74. Chekhov's letter of March 5, 1889 to A. S. Souvorin refers to Dostoevsky: 'good, but immodest, pretentious.' Quoted in Thomas Mann, *Last Essays*, translated by Tania and James Stern. London. Secker and Warburg, 1959, p. 200.

[3] Eliot's Introduction to Father William Tiverton, *D. H. Lawrence and Human Existence*. London. Rockliff, 1951, p. vii.

[4] *Form and Value in Modern Poetry*, p. 255.

the 'centrifugal impulse of heresy', set against the orthodoxy which he himself avowed. But the charge can hardly be said to mean much: or rather, it is inadmissible because based as much upon hearsay, lore, gossip, and Middleton Murry's reminiscences of Lawrence as upon the evidence of the novels and stories. Lawrence could defeat the charge by saying that he regards as characteristics what Eliot regards as crimes. But the second charge is more particular, that Lawrence 'wished to go as low as possible in the scale of human consciousness, in order to find something that he could assure himself was *real*'.[1] Put like that, the charge hardly requires an answer: a writer is entitled to go wherever he likes, in the scale of human consciousness, to find what he can register as real. Still, we know what Eliot has in mind; passages in such books as *Mornings in Mexico* and *Etruscan Places*, in which Lawrence seems infatuated with forms of life merely because they come low in the scale of consciousness; like the Hopi snake-dance. But I don't think Lawrence ever proposed that such images should be the end or object of human life; he admired them as a basis for a new beginning, a recourse to the roots of human life, where the gap between nature and culture is small, but still distinguishable. And if a writer proposes to start again, he is well advised to start with the human body and the earth. He will not end there, but his search for subsequent recognitions and more complex stages of development must never lose the sense of their origin.

But Eliot's most vehement quarrel with Lawrence is on the question of morality. In *After Strange Gods* he says that Lawrence's characters 'betray no respect for, or even awareness of, moral obligations, and seem to be unfurnished with even the most commonplace kind of conscience'.[2] It is certainly true of Lawrence's major heroines and heroes that they are not troubled by any official morality of choices and decisions, they act by their own freedom, they are not attentive to laws of church, state, or society.

---

[1] John Baillie and Hugh Martin (editors), *Revelation*, by Gustaf Aulen, Karl Barth, Sergius Bulgakoff, M. C. D'Arcy, T. S. Eliot, Walter M. Horton, and William Temple. London. Faber and Faber, 1937, p. 32.

[2] T. S. Eliot, *After Strange Gods: A Primer of Modern Heresy*. London. Faber and Faber, 1934, p. 37.

The opposition they recognize comes from the nature of the demand, their own demand for fulfilment; it is intrinsic to their desire, they recognize no other authority. They do not admit, as a critical law to be obeyed, any voice but their own. They demand that their lives be transfigured, and that the miracle take place in terms of their relations to themselves or to others, other men, other women. What such characters ask of each other is that they open the gates upon infinity, the sublime. Since this is an utterly private experience, the question of a moral law is not deemed to arise. These characters do not admit any recognition of society as such, or values arising, with any claim to force, from the fact of community: other people are given about the same attention as the cyclist who comes upon the quarrelling Birkin and Ursula in the 'Excurse' chapter of *Women in Love*, they stay quiet for a few seconds until he goes away. The question of conscience is overwhelmed by the consideration of self-determination, self-fulfilment. I am not sure that these charges can be answered. The Eliot of *After Strange Gods* believed that the moral law was absolute, and that it must take precedence over all other considerations, at whatever cost. Lawrence believed that there was no such thing as a moral absolute, and that the fundamental issue was the relation between one person and another, as an extension of the relation between that person and himself. The only morality his characters acknowledge is the morality of the right relation. In that setting, morality, so far as it is embodied in the promptings of conscience or natural or moral law, is merely an administrative device, no better than any other and no worthier to be obeyed. Success in Lawrence's world means that the characters for whom he cares have brought themselves or brought each other to a satisfactory moment in the action of their lives. Moral questions or considerations which come from outside these relationships do not arise.

Take, for instance, *The Captain's Doll*, one of Lawrence's most convincing stories in the sense that the reader is easily brought to believe in the several characters, their motives and personalities. It is convincing, too, by virtue of Lawrence's remarkable power in securing, on behalf of the characters who deserve such treatment, an impression of their significance as being more than the sum of its appearances. In the case of Captain Hepburn, the reader has no difficulty in registering him as a most formidable presence, a man of continuous if somewhat alien force, even when he is absent from the scene of the story: he is indelible. The question of the relation between Captain Hepburn and Countess zu Rassentlow is the supreme question of the story, and in comparison with that, the relation between the Captain and his wife is secondary, useful only for the light it throws upon the principal relation. The process by which Captain Hepburn and the Countess are at last brought together, after their first meetings and partings, is meant to engage the reader's full concern: he is meant to follow, with full recognition of the issues involved, the subtle alterations of mood and feeling in both characters. The alterations in the Countess's feeling are much greater than in the Captain's; the story implies that he is under no obligation to change, but merely to cause a change in her. The last pages, in which the Countess is brought to change her life and to accept the stern conditions of love which the Captain imposes, are wonderfully done, the reader cannot help but feel the pressure increase, and consign his own feeling to the Captain's power. Much of Lawrence's power is engaged in the Captain's behalf; the reader hardly realises the extent to which he has been affected. It requires a considerable effort on his part to disengage himself from the rhetoric of the story to the extent of recognizing something monstrous as well as something magnificent in the Captain. The reader feels that he is being wilful if he asks, of the relation between the Captain and the Countess at the end, such questions as these: is there any place, in such a relation, for the Captain's two children, cast off in boarding schools? Does the Captain feel at all sad or guilty for the waste of his wife's life, such as it was? Is it entirely obtuse to regard the Captain as a moral gangster?

What I have been saying is merely a gloss on Eliot's critique of Lawrence, but the strain between the two writers is far more fundamental than the gloss can say. The differences of temper are nearly endless; between Eliot, who secreted poems as if they were the recently discovered work of Language rather than the recently declared work of a man called Eliot: and Lawrence, who consigned everything to the fable of his time, proffering himself as his major work, compounded diversely of choices, chances, works, and days. Eliot could not have written the 'Water-Party' chapter of *Women in Love*; nor could Lawrence have written 'Gerontion', 'Marina', *The Waste Land* or *Four Quartets*. I risk these banal sentences to say something more worthwhile which arises from the comparison: it is essential to Eliot's life as well as to his art that he should say, with full normative intention, 'Humility is endless': it is no less essential to Lawrence's life and art that he would have found the noun in that sentence contemptible. But I must try to go a little further with the comparison, not in the hope of saying anything at all adequate to Eliot's achievement in poetry, but to take the weight of it, in any comparison we might make with Lawrence. Here are the opening lines of 'Burnt Norton', and I choose them as representing not by any means the entire range of Eliot's poetry but the most characteristic of its later directions:

> Time present and time past
> Are both perhaps present in time future,
> And time future contained in time past.
> If all time is eternally present
> All time is unredeemable.
> What might have been is an abstraction
> Remaining a perpetual possibility
> Only in a world of speculation.
> What might have been and what has been
> Point to one end, which is always present.
> Footfalls echo in the memory
> Down the passage which we did not take
> Towards the door we never opened
> Into the rose-garden. My words echo
> Thus, in your mind.
> But to what purpose
> Disturbing the dust on a bowl of rose-leaves
> I do not know.
> Other echoes
> Inhabit the garden. Shall we follow?
> Quick, said the bird, find them, find them,
> Round the corner. Through the first gate,
> Into our first world, shall we follow

The deception of the thrush? Into our first world.
There they were, dignified, invisible,
Moving without pressure, over the dead leaves,
In the autumn heat, through the vibrant air,
And the bird called, in response to
The unheard music hidden in the shrubbery,
And the unseen eyebeam crossed, for the roses
Had the look of flowers that are looked at.
There they were as our guests, accepted and accepting.
So we moved, and they, in a formal pattern,
Along the empty alley, into the box circle,
To look down into the drained pool.
Dry the pool, dry concrete, brown edged,
And the pool was filled with water out of sunlight,
And the lotos rose, quietly, quietly,
The surface glittered out of heart of light,
And they were behind us, reflected in the pool.
Then a cloud passed, and the pool was empty.
Go, said the bird, for the leaves were full of children,
Hidden excitedly, containing laughter.
Go, go, go, said the bird: human kind
Cannot bear very much reality.
Time past and time future
What might have been and what has been
Point to one end, which is always present.[1]

It is well known that in the summer of 1934 Eliot visited a ruined mansion in Gloucestershire, and walked in its deserted garden: the house occupied the site of an earlier house which had been burnt two hundred years before. It is a fact only less familiar that Eliot, in an autobiographical lecture in St. Louis in 1959, spoke of another deserted garden which may have meant even more to him than the garden at Burnt Norton. When he was a boy in St. Louis, he lived in a house on Locust Street beside a girls' school called the Mary Institute. The school was founded by the poet's grandfather, the Reverend William Greenleaf Eliot, and it was named after the

---

[1] T. S. Eliot, *Collected Poems 1909–1962*. London. Faber and Faber, 1963, pp. 189–190.

founder's daughter Mary. From the Eliot home, the schoolgirls could be seen playing next door in the schoolyard, and Eliot recalls that he was allowed to go into the schoolyard, but only when the girls had gone. Once, however, he went into the yard before the last girls had left: he looked in a window, and saw a girl looking out at him, and he fled.[1] So the playground acquired a strange resonance for him, being a place of young girls, echoes, presences, and absences. Clearly, it will not injure the poetry of 'Burnt Norton' if we recite the lore of these gardens, because the passage quoted is in no sense a description of a garden; though I am ready to believe that both gardens played some part in the imaginative process which led to the composition. The passage is not a description, Eliot is not interested in making the reader see the rose-garden, he is using language in such a manner that things are recognized, by its means, rather than seen. The words act 'to compel the recognition they precede'. It is not characteristic of Eliot's poetry, despite *Sweeney Agonistes* and the public-house scene in *The Waste Land*, to make upon an event the demand of immediacy; least of all that kind of immediacy or intensity in which the chief instigation comes from the perceiver's will, and the event is largely an excuse for the release of will-power. The moments of rapture in Eliot's poems are those in which the individual will plays very little part: the soul recognizes the conditions of rapture, but it does not demand them. The only cherished form of intensity is that of recognition, a profound movement of feeling to rise to the occasion. It is never a matter of desire, desire is voided so that the purity of recognition may be complete. The appropriate comparison is with the procedures of Shakespeare's last plays, and especially of that scene which Eliot regarded as the greatest of all recognition scenes in Shakespeare, the restoration of Marina to Pericles. The comparison is valid because the scene gives the intensity of recognition as a process, starting all the way back with Pericles blank and speechless, and

---

[1] Cf. Walter J. Ong, "Burnt Norton" in St. Louis', *American Literature,* Vol. XXXIII, No. 4, January 1962, pp. 522–6. The lecture was delivered on November 11, 1959.

going all the way through doubt and faith to the rapture of certainty when Pericles cannot withhold belief and the 'sea of joy' rushes upon him while he hears the music of the spheres. Correspondingly, Eliot's art in the later poems is not a matter of local intensities but of processes of recognition. Facts are given, but given as if their chief privilege were to participate in a particularly subtle music made possible by their humility. Events are presented, but presented as if seen from a distance, so that we see not merely each event but its relation to other events. Words are recited, but as if the chief delight of one word were in leading to the next: they issue from feelings which have detached themselves from anything as rough-and-ready as emotions or desires. Each word serves the pattern, the grand cadence of the passage, directing the reader's mind forward as if to receive, in the fifth Act, another Marina. This kind of poetry is not preoccupied with events as such, but with the relation between palpable sounds and a correspondingly 'unheard' music: the intensity of palpable sounds is not their criterion. In the present passage the unheard music may be received as the music of absence or of 'what might have been', and I find it impossible to distinguish it from Absolute Music, as in Keats's invocation to 'heard melodies' and 'those unheard'. The unseen eyebeam is the visual equivalent of an 'absence in reality', recovered now by memory and association, one vision invoking another. In the organization of the poem, such tokens of rapture are probably nine parts illusion to one part apprehension, and that is the nature of their power. 'What might have been' stands for Absolute Being, and the words register the speaker's sense of it, or the loss of it: it has the same grammatical status as unheard music and unseen eyebeams. The point to make is that in Eliot's later poems what is registered is never that thing merely, or the same thing promoted to vehemence: it is always crossed by another light coming from a long distance, as if its being registered as itself, with whatever force, were not enough. If we approach a rose-garden through passages we do not take and doors we have never opened, the place is an area of feeling as much as an area of horticulture; it is an ablative estate, created as much by feelings of loss and possibility as by the gardener's hand. The first effect is that our response to these words is never allowed to vent itself upon a scene presented for its own sake or with a view to intensity as the main require-ment. The words fend us off, as much as they compel our attention; they are a veil through which we are allowed to see, but the veil prevents us from laying rude hands upon the object of vision. The ideal reader is then in the state of consciousness which Eliot certifies in the next passage of 'Burnt Norton':

> The inner freedom from the practical desire,
> The release from action and suffering, release from the inner
> And the outer compulsion, yet surrounded
> By a grace of sense, a white light still and moving,
> *Erhebung* without motion . . .

In that state of consciousness, the words we speak, like the first passage in 'Burnt Norton', have an air of speaking themselves: they issue from a source which does not assert itself beyond the degree of voice or presence.

It will hardly be denied that Eliot, speaking from such a world, was hostile to the Promethean spirit, even in its relatively mild forms. He seems to have thought of Prometheans as barbarians, either in Santayana's sense or in Blackmur's; in the one, the barbarian is 'the man who regards his passions as their own excuse for being',[1] and Santayana had Browning and Whitman in mind; in the other, 'the barbarians are those outside us whom we are tempted to follow when we would escape ourselves', and Black-mur had Whitman and Pound in mind, both 'good poets when we ourselves wish to be fragmentary'.[2] The names do not matter. Eliot even found it possible to rebuke Henry James in this spirit for not toning down 'the absurdities of Roderick's sculpture' in *Roderick Hudson*, 'the pathetic Thirst and the gigantic Adam'. In that novel, James 'too much identifies himself with Rowland, does not see through the solemnity he has created in that character, commits the cardinal sin of failing to "detect" one of his own

---

[1] George Santayana, *Interpretations of Poetry and Religion*. New York. Harper and Row, 1957, p. 176.

[2] R. P. Blackmur, *Anni Mirabiles*, p. 33.

characters'.[1] It is a condition of Lawrence's art that the writer gives his characters as much freedom as they demand, and the benefit of every doubt. Eliot thought him irresponsible, the Prometheanism rampant.

Eliot's critique of Lawrence and of Blake goes far beyond those writers; it presses hard as a principled suspicion upon Promethean motives in general. Indeed, it stands for nearly everything that can be said against Prometheans: a more elaborate prosecution would merely work out Eliot's implications and apply them at large. Of course in the treating of any ostensible 'advance' in the means of culture, it is always possible to present its limitations as radical defects, its accidental qualities as substance: thus Lévi-Strauss in *Tristes tropiques* proposes a relation of cause and effect between the art of alphabetical writing and the exploitation of man by man. By an equally extreme argument, one could say that Prometheus was an interfering busybody, the cause of all our woes, and his gift in poor taste; though it would be impossible to hold that opinion without having accepted the gift and entertained the donor. Such all-or-nothing arguments are beside the point. Even if we take the weight of Eliot's critique, it should not force us beyond the point of looking somewhat ruefully at Promethean motives, and at the bench of desolation from which we survey them. If Prometheus is compromised, it is because his followers have taken to the habit of enjoying their transgression and making of their original sin a deeply cherished illness. Or it is because Zeus has been humiliated, his majesty domesticated. In either of these versions we are moving from epic and tragedy to irony and comedy, as if from *Moby-Dick* to *Pierre*, or from Mann's *Dr. Faustus* to *Felix Krull*. By a turn of the screw, heroes become buffoons and tricksters. But the most probable fate is that heroes and villains are tamed, their violence assimilated to bourgeois norms. This is the fate reserved for them in Ransom's poem, 'Prometheus in Straits'.

Prometheus is presented as surveying the world which he made possible by theft of knowledge: the several stanzas show him visit-

---

[1] T. S. Eliot, 'Henry James: The Hawthorne Aspect', *Little Review*, Vol. V, No. 4, August 1918, pp. 47–53.

ing the academies, where his beneficiaries are busy with the intellectual pursuits which have established themselves, as for instance a political conference, a class in Art Appreciation, a seminar. Prometheus is displeased: on all sides, he hears talk for the sake of talk, twitterings, exegeses; all the magnificent powers contained in his gift are domesticated, he finds. Zeus is addressed as if he were an Assistant Professor, doubtful about his tenure:

> The prophet is solicited before he has well thundered
> And escapes with credit if he do not turn disciple.

Ransom has always wanted his gods to thunder, and he has rebuked those men, nearly everyone now, who takes their gods as images of themselves and find the thunder charming. Religion, history, poetry: each is domesticated, its harm taken away in bourgeois trifles, theories, interpretations, symbols. In the last stanza Prometheus runs away from chattering men who are not really concerned with 'the due distinctions of faith and fact and fiction':

> I will go somewhere by a streamside abounding with granite
> And but little human history and dereliction;
> To the Unknown Man I will raise an altar upon it
> And comfort my knees with bruises of genuflection.[1]

Perhaps Zeus was right, who had in mind letting the human race run out like an obsolete model. In any event, here we have a gently ironic poet bringing the good thief to his knees.

---

[1] John Crowe Ransom, *Selected Poems*. New York. Knopf, 1964, pp. 33-4.